My Emerald Leaf, Paradise Within:

Living a Life of Prayer

A Selection of Poems,
Hymn Texts,
and Prayer Stories

Sandy Smyth

www.xulonpress.com

June 5, 2012

Judy,
Blessings on your journey, my friend!

Love,
Sandy

TABLE OF CONTENTS

FOREWORD

Recently I entered a guided meditation that led me to a bonfire surrounded by a sacred circle of friends. I was asked by our leader to toss my held grief into the fire and let it go.

What emerged from the fire was a green leaf with the message, "Follow the Emerald Leaf." The Emerald Leaf is an image in one of my 2011 poems and, for me, symbolizes eco-spirituality, my authentic self grounded in natural beauty and God's Spirit.

For me, natural beauty draws me into closer relationship with the Holy Spirit and to wholeness. Wholeness, I believe, is the desired state of being in which we experience the joy of Heaven on Earth—moments of deep communion in which we are in complete harmony with God, ourselves, and the entire creation to experience what I call *"Paradise Within."*

This little book is a collection of my poems, hymn texts, and stories of answered fervent prayer—not only my prayers, but also prayers shared by friends and acquaintances of faith. They are a testimony of how the Holy Spirit works in the life of the faithful who pray without ceasing and who undergo mystical experiences as ordinary persons.

My poems, hymn texts, and stories of prayer express deep grief and questioning as well as great joy. They arise out of communion with the Holy Spirit who listens to the concerns of my heart, often when I am the most broken, and through nature inspires my writing.

In 2010, I published these poems and hymn texts in a book titled *Journey to Wholeness through the Creative Arts*. My intent then was to inspire readers to express their emotional responses to the imagery in the poems by making art. My intent now is to simply share poems and stories that celebrate living a life of prayer and to inspire readers to welcome into their lives the gift of the Holy Spirit who desires our becoming a new creation in Christ.

Blessings,
Sandy Smyth
2012

INTRODUCTION

In I Thessalonians 5:17, Jesus tells us to pray without ceasing. He tells us to ask boldly in His name, and our prayers will be answered. As we know, our prayers are not always answered as we see fit. There are those faithful, like Job, who feel that God never answers them. But Jesus also says in Matthew 6:8 that God knows our hearts and our needs even before we do and that whatever we ask in His name will be granted (John 14:13–14; Romans 8:26–27).

From my experience, to pray without ceasing means to be in a trusting, ongoing, *responsive* relationship with the Holy Spirit, such as a young child would be with a loving parent (Mark 10:15–16). So that when a true need arises and the person who is in that trusting relationship asks God for help, particularly when that person prays with others who are also in such a relationship with the Holy Spirit, God listens (Matthew 21:22, 11:24; I Peter 3:12; Judith 4:13; Sirach 3:5; James 5:13, 15, 16).

If patient, they will eventually see how the Holy Spirit responds to that prayer in a sequence of events that (the very God who hears and loves us and wants us to become whole beings) brings about revelations and solutions through meaningful coincidences or what we call "God-incidences." Famous analytical psychologist Carl Jung defined these meaningful coincidences as synchronicity.

Why Pray?

Scripture tells us that God knows our thoughts, our wounds, our needs, and our desires, and He wants us to become whole as new creatures in Christ. So why pray without ceasing?

If to pray without ceasing means to be in a trusting, ongoing, responsive relationship with the Holy Spirit, then that relationship requires meditative quiet time apart for listening to a God who responds in a still, small voice as the Holy Spirit (Jude 1:20). We know that still, small voice from that of others as a sheep knows its shepherd (John 10:1–21).

But how can we be sure that we hear the right voice when we listen to God in prayer? We hear the voice of our wounds and egos and pleasures all day long, but when we settle down into the quiet to rest in God's Spirit, the Shepherd's voice is distinct from the rest.

Scripture tell us Jesus would not leave us as orphans but would send His Spirit as our guide and counselor (John 14:15–31).

The intention of the Holy Spirit is that we become whole in spirit through love and compassion; that we first love God with all our hearts and minds; and second, love our neighbors *as ourselves* (Matthew 22:34–40). The Shepherd's voice will always move us toward wholeness and agapeic action or acts of God's grace working in and through us to others in need.

One of my favorite quotes is from nineteenth century author Ralph Waldo Trine, who said in his 1898 classic *In Tune with the Infinite*, still published today, that:

We can enter into the quiet of our own interior selves … all things that it is valuable for us to know will come to us if we will but open ourselves to the voice of Spirit [of Infinite Wisdom]. (pp. 108–109)

Trine calls this voice the interior guide, the voice of the

Higher Self, conscience, or intuition (p. 106). Regarding the danger of a harmful intuition, Trine says:

We need not be afraid of this, however, for the voice of the soul, this voice of God speaking through the soul, will never direct one to do harm to anyone, nor to do anything that is not in accordance with the highest standards of right, truth and justice. And if you at anytime have a prompting of his kind, know that it is not the voice of intuition, it is some characteristic of your lower self that is prompting you. (pp. 107–108)

We hear the Shepherd's voice when we become still, apart from the fray of the world's busy-ness. Jesus took time apart to pray, to listen to God (Matthew 14:23), and to know God's will. Just as Jesus exemplified, we should pray without ceasing to keep our hearts and minds open to the Holy Spirit's guidance and will, which is Love.

Christian mystic Evelyn Underhill, author of *Concerning the Inner Life,* published in 1926, says of inner and outer life:

There must be two movements which must be plainly present in every spiritual life. The energy of its prayer [movement] must be directed on the one hand towards God; and on the other towards men. The first movement embraces the whole range of spiritual communion between the soul and God; in it we turn towards Divine Reality in adoration, bathing, so to speak, our souls in the Eternal Light. In the second, we return, with the added peace and energy thus gained, to the natural world; there to do spiritual work for and with God for other men. (pp. 51–51)

In touch, through meditative, centering prayer with the Divine Ground of Being (Tillich) at our core, we form a relationship of trust with the Holy Spirit, so that as we listen to her still small voice, we not only channel agapeic love to ourselves and others, we become co-creative with her (Romans 8). The collection of stories in this little book is proof that God listens to the focused, fervent prayers of the faithful. Unlike atheists in Colorado who have posted on billboards, "God is an imaginary friend," to the faithful, God is powerfully present to us in prayer life (even if we *feel* God is absent) and through the compassionate presence and actions of others.

The stories in the first section illustrate the power of focused prayer. But before I share these stories, I want to define focused prayer. During one of Deepak Chopra's lectures on the power of positive thought or focused intent to bring about positive change, I made the connection between the power of prayer and the power of focused intention and asked him, as he was leaving the podium, whether focused intent was the same as prayer. He said yes.

What he meant was that the energy of our thoughts attract particles in the universe to cause meaningful coincidences (synchronicity) to occur, which is why it is so important to think positively to create a positive reality. Deepak's exact words on his website are: "Your focused intentions set the infinite organizing power of the universe in motion. Trust that infinite organizing power to orchestrate the complete fulfillment of your desires."

I believe that the "infinite organizing power of the universe" is the Spirit of God who hears and answers the prayers of the faithful. While discussion of quantum physics is beyond the scope of this book, the science of faith may well be of interest to the reader. Hopefully, it is enough here for the reader to know that focused intention is focused thought is focused prayer (I Corinthians 14:15). How so?

When we pray, our thoughts are focused on a subject that concerns us. By focusing our attention on what concerns us, we draw attention to it, particularly when two or three faithful are gathered in prayer; and, I believe, God hears and attends to those concerns of the heart (Matthew 18:20). I also believe that the Holy Spirit activates solutions through a series of God-incidences or encounters with others who manifest grace, support, and wisdom during our times of crisis. Often our encounters are with strangers who we later consider to be angels as we look back on our grievous situations. I believe God is with us through others, human and non (by "non" I mean non-human such as pets and nature).

The following prayer stories in Part I, III, and V illustrate the power of fervent, focused prayer of the faithful who are living a Life of Prayer. The poems in Part II and hymn texts in Part IV reveal my thoughts and feelings while in cherished prayer time with God in my ongoing journey to wholeness.

PART I.

MY ANSWERED PRAYER STORIES

Mother's Cat Finds a Home

Elmo's story illustrates the power of focused prayer and faith in a God who desires our wholeness.

My 90-year-old mother was moved from her home in Florida to a hospice facility where she lived. Because I lived in Connecticut and my younger sister lived in Texas, we were operating as a tag team, monitoring and caring for our mother from afar, making frequent trips back and forth to Florida to visit her and take care of her personal business. Fortunately, mother was blessed to have a competent and compassionate caregiver, which eased our agony of not being able to care for her up close. So our main concern at the time was finding the right home for mother's beloved companion, her orange tabby, Elmo.

Elmo was a loving, loyal, 12-year-old cat in good health. He had great big blue-green eyes and watched mother religiously as he sat beside her on the hospital bed in her living room. They were inseparable. Hospice was caring for mother at home at the time. We all loved Elmo but could not take him into one of our homes.

I became ill with worry about his demise and began to pray about it. I asked my prayer team at church to pray for Elmo. We prayed for weeks, before mother was transported to the hospice facility, that Elmo would find a loving home. We got no responses until one day, a hospice worker, whose

20-year-old cat had just died, went on the Internet to the hospice website where my sister had just posted Elmo's picture and description. The woman had been praying that a cat would find her. Her cat had had big blue-green eyes and was an orange tabby just like Elmo. She missed her cat companion terribly, but when she saw Elmo, the match was made in heaven, as they say! Certainly I believe it was!

When I met the woman while visiting my mother, who was still at home, I was stunned to see how kind she was and how well she interacted with Elmo. Mother was so relieved that she was able to let her baby go to his new home and move on. Elmo adapted well after the first week. Mother would not have been able to leave her home peacefully for the hospice facility had Elmo not been adopted by this angel who took him into her home and loved him.

My sister, mother, and I could not believe how wonderful this turn of events was for a cat that seemed to have a grim future in a shelter. I was no longer ill with worry because I realized that God heard the fervent prayers made for my mother, my sister, Elmo, and me, made by me and my prayer team at church. So much planning regarding my mother's placement, caregivers, sale of her car, and cleaning out of her home and its eventual sale went smoothly that I know the Holy Spirit worked through human angels who were there for us in that time of crisis as a result of fervent, focused prayer.

One more "meaningful coincidence" happened on the way to mother's memorial service at the cemetery. As two of her best friends were riding together to the service, the locks on their car doors kept going up and down. They felt that mother was with them in spirit the whole ride!

Ash Creek

In 1993, my husband and I were going through a difficult

time, reconciling after a year of separation. My place of comfort was the park at Ash Creek where I would walk with our dog on a path that eventually led out to a broad view of Long Island Sound. I was taking religion courses at a local university and becoming familiar with the experiences of the mystics of the world's major religions.

As a Christian, I knew my own religion as the way of Jesus Christ. But I was beginning to wonder why God was just as real to those of different faiths. I had recently attended a church service where a large painting of Jesus sitting on a rock with his arms outstretched to me, and to every other person in the pews around me, hung in the sanctuary high on the wall behind the pulpit. It was Jesus as he might have looked in the Middle Eastern culture of his day.

The painting was very comforting to me as I reflected on the trying state of my marriage. I was also concerned about a friend of mine who was recently divorced and dating men I considered questionable, meaning they didn't have her best interest at heart. I felt she was looking for love in all the wrong places, as the song goes, and that she might get into a dangerous situation.

One morning on a kind of labyrinth walk with my dog at Ash Creek, I kept asking the Holy Spirit to show me who God was. I had been keeping a prayer journal during this difficult time, always praying for my marriage to heal from the pain of our year of separation which became a time of great suffering from a series of losses. At that time I drew very close to God who seemed to be my only companion, God and my dog.

So when God heard my prayer asking for God to reveal Himself/Herself to me, the answer came as I was walking out to the point to view the sound. I walked deep in worrisome thought with my head facing the ground. When I looked up, a stranger was walking toward me who resembled the picture of Jesus in the sanctuary of the church I had recently attended.

As he got closer, I felt this incredible compassion for me. At the same time, I felt an equally incredible release of love burst forth from my heart with a knowing that all would be well; not only for me, a Christian, but also for every one of faith and those who seemed most lost. I have never experienced the intensity of that moment again, but I am very aware of the Presence who loves me regardless of my failings (Romans 8:38, 39).

My Dog Is Missing

When my sister came for her usual fall visit to Connecticut to escape the heat of Houston and to enjoy the colors of the season, we would walk my dog through the woods that bordered the lake a mile or so from our house. No leash was necessary since dogs were allowed to walk freely on the paths that circled the lake, but they had to be accompanied by their guardians.

That summer I had introduced my little dog to the creek that led into the lake so that I knew she could handle the current if she wanted to swim. She didn't really like the water, so I wasn't too concerned that she might get caught in the current after a heavy rain. A waterfall flowed into the creek, and I loved to stand on the bridge that connected one side of the creek that was level with the parking area and the other that rose up a steep hill.

The day that my sister and I walked with my dog across the bridge and up the steep hill was blue, clear, and crisp. We were having a lovely time chatting and my dog was close to her side. Suddenly, three large German shepherds came out of nowhere and my dog took off. For what seemed like an hour we searched for her, called her, and were terrified she might have been caught up by the creek's current, which was strong that day. My sister and I split up to go in opposite directions. I was so distraught that I leaned against a tree and became very still. My knees were weak and I almost fell to the ground. God heard the groaning of my heart and gave me a picture in my mind of where she had gone.

I felt some relief, but I still called out. Finally my sister returned, upset that our dog hadn't been found. I told her about the picture in my mind, so we went back down the hill and over the bridge and back to our car and waited while I called my husband to come help us find her. When he drove up a half hour later, out the window he called, "Are you missing something?" then rolled down the back window. There in the back seat, poking her head out the window and very happy to see us, was our dog! Since we lived several miles away from the area we had been walking her, I asked him how in the world he found her. He said he'd gotten a call from someone who lived near where we had been who found our dog on her back porch.

I described the picture in my head and it turned out to be very accurate, yet we still don't know exactly which house she went to. She had run down the hill when the German shepherds came after her, had crossed over the raging creek, gone back to the car, left footprints on the car (which I failed to see), then ran up a hill to a neighborhood of big houses and sat on a back porch. That was the picture God gave me when I rested against the tree, needing God's help and praying without words, just a very heavy heart.

Stephen's Story: Planting

The reason I want to share Stephen's story here is because it speaks to how God touches us through nature, as my poems reflect, regardless of our religious orientation. Stephen has been called by the Holy Spirit to be an Episcopal priest since he experienced God in Assisi. It is a gift to know him. He has rekindled my interest in eco-spirituality and Christian ministry. His following story is about "Planting":

In my family when I was growing up, no one went to church, we never talked about God, and we didn't read the Bible. I learned the Lord's Prayer only because it was recited at third-grade public school assemblies (how times have changed!); I was puzzled by this other "pledge of allegiance" that everyone knew except me, so I just mouthed some words to fit in. Despite this beginning, though, somehow the Word of God was planted in my soul many years ago and grew in secret, waiting till it was time to emerge.

I think the planting happened in Assisi, the home of St. Francis, the summer I was 15 years old. We had spent a year living in Italy while my dad was on a research sabbatical. Near the end of our time there, my parents and I drove to Assisi, which my mother really wanted to see. After a brief tour around the church to see the frescoes, I left my parents to admire the art and architecture (boring) while I went outdoors. I wandered upward through the town till I stumbled upon a path that climbed up the ridge of a steep hill above the town, along the ruins of an old fortress wall. Up there, by myself, looking down upon the cathedral and the town, something happened. I felt it, I knew it, but I couldn't describe it. Something happened.

I didn't have language for it, and the experience remains a mystery, but somehow I walked into a non-ordinary state of being, there on the mountainside. Now, I would say I was opened to an experience of God. Somehow, I was called up that ridge and my soul was opened just enough for a little word to be planted.

I think that seed germinated and grew as a calling to work for the Earth, to befriend and care for our brothers and sisters in all of Creation, which became the work of the first half of my life. As the seedling continued to grow, perhaps that container was no longer large enough and I was called to the mountain again to break open the old pot and allow the root-bound seedling room to grow and flourish anew in a fuller and richer life in Christ and in the Church. I do wonder what the grower has in mind next! Aren't seeds miraculous?

PART II.

POEMS 1961 TO 2012

PARADISE WITHIN

INTIMATE EARTH
INTIMATE SPIRIT

A selection of poems
from 1961 to the present

At first, I ran by the creek;
At last, the creek ran through me.

by
Sandy Smyth
©1993–2008

FREEDOM

That I could live among the trees,
Breathe the breath of Nature
Through my pores;
And sweep in gracious ecstasy and ease,
Like wind that passes inward
From the shores.

1961

THE YOUNG GIRL

Her heart is like unbridled wind,
The spirit of the auburn colt
Who canters across the leas
And leaps into restless streams.

Her thoughts are like the purple bird
Who sweeps away into the sunset,
Through cloud-like dreams,
And soars among the stars.

Her ties are but the bond of blood;
Her life belongs but to the wild,
Her beauty the blush of nature's truth,
She, half mature and half a child.

1961

NIRVANA

The Wind blew evening from her flute,
And through the pale pure dusk,
She swept a teakwood bird aloft,
In gracious ecstasy and ease,
High through deep green leaves of thought,
Somewhere betwixt the Moon and Dust,
To move incorporeal, like a Star.

1964

RESTLESSNESS

Within my very essence
Burns a longing,
Restless,
Restrained,
And unfulfilled;
Weeping,
As tears of early morn
Appear upon warm woods,
Who mourn
Not knowing why.

1964

A CONTRAST

The wolf and the loon
Call and howl
From desolate places,
Lit by a cold
And abandoning Moon.

Their kin, duck and dog,
Bark and quack
Midst a ring
Of on-looking faces,
Lit by a warm
And accepting sun.

1965

THE ICE STORM

Night came down a frozen rain,
Clinging clearly to the leafless trees;
The cold, clear creek
Moved free and deep
Through a hall all glacier clear,
Where brilliant pine green chandeliers,
Ring tingling in the wind,
Made a palace of the crystal dark.

(Morning):

The sun rings round the crystal morn,
Bursting wooden pipes
Beneath the ice.

1964

THE MUSE

The Moon followed me home
One night through the wood,
And it stood half-hid
Behind trees, as I stopped
To cross a cold creek
Or a stump in the dark.
Like a dog, it followed me home,
And lay waiting for me
When I got there.

1965

THE CONTENDERS

Two squirrels whirl down
A tree and around,
Each holding for life
To his brittle bough;
'Til the chase beats one
To the splintered ground,
And the other halts...
Startled and staring down.

Two bucks clash on a cliff
'Til horns interlock,
Each holding for life
To his clumsy rock;
'Til the sport beats one
To the splintered ground,
And the other halts...
Startled and staring down.

Two cocks circle a roof,
All talon and claw,
Each holding for life
To his patch of straw;
'Til the fight beats one
To the splintered ground,
And the other halts...
Startled and staring down.

Two lovers stand firm
Across a room steel-still,
Each holding for life
To his own free will;

continued

41

'Til a push shoves one
To the splintered ground,
And the other halts...
Startled and staring down.

1966

THE SHELL

The waves left an array
Of shells up on the sand.
I picked one up and
Fondled it in my hand.
And lifting it to my ear to hear
The thrilling pounding of the sea,
I overheard the echo of a Soul
Far lonelier than me.

1969

THE DEATH

Her stroke was a shock;
But we had a few moments
Before she fell a final sleep.

I begged her to fight with death;
But she withdrew in horror
At the thought of living.

She smiled like a soft-faced child,
And babbled in breaths
Beneath the mask,
When I closed her hands
About a rock
She always prayed on.

She winked, blue-clear
As a planet on a frozen night
Before she left her body sleeping.

The funeral was simple;
Greens and bittersweet
Lay over the coffin.
I never cried,
While others were weeping,

For I felt the presence
Of a precious guest
Back in the house.
I was a happy awhile,
But now I have nightmares.

1971

THE SANCTUARY

Wind,
Take me down to a quiet glen
Where I will never
Hear the crowds again,
So I can hear the voiceless noise
Of blowing trees,
And the delicate chatter
Of scattering leaves.

Take me to the edge of creeks,
Where wet air splatters
On my hair and cheeks,
And the rush of weightless diamonds
Flow over my aching feet.

Take me where the water goes,
And lay me down upon a rock,
Where I may never see a clock
To tell me of my wasted hours
Of too much doing.

Drop the petals of precious flowers
Around me for my viewing;
For when the Moon's shadows
Round me creep,
The world will find me
In a beauteous sleep
Deep within its Natural Soul.

1972

LISTEN TO THE SOUND

Listen to the sound the Moon makes,
As she slips into a mountain stream
And slides like a silver snake
Down through the leafless woods,
And slithers, glistening over stones,
Coiling into quiet pools,
Deep beneath the pine-fast cliffs,
Where one can hear
The piercing undertones of Silence.

1972

TOUCH

The joy that rises up in me
When I touch my love,
Also rises up in me
When he is touched
By lovely things:
I feel joy when leafy branches
Blow across his brow;
Joy, when drops of sweat
Slide down his cheek;
Joy, when the Wind
Loosens his hair
And inner song;
Joy, when he walks
Along the creek
And throws stones back up
At the waterfall.

Am I all the lovely things
That touch him?
Then why do I feel no joy
When he is touched
By a lovely woman?

1972

WOULD THAT THE
WAY OF DEATH

Would that the way of death
Could be our choosing,
Unique as our most
Cherished fantasy,
Life's last blessing.

No shocking, crashing,
Writhing, thrashing death;
But to expire as gently
As natural breath,
The untold self unfold;

That death would descend
Like a soft white Dove,
Whose wings would enfold
Like the petals of
A smooth white rose;
And soar me to vast heights
My soul has longed for
All my heavy life.

1973

EQUILIBRIUM

Puking, perspiring,
Tears of laughing and crying;
Creating pages and paintings
Of thoughts inspiring;
Are ways the self purges,
Purifies and rescues itself
From dying or going mad.

When we are pure, we are free
To walk on the center line.
Through life, we experience
Each side of the balance beam:
We totter on
Between love and hate,
Security and fear,
Joy and sorrow,
And so on, from year to year.

1974

ABSTRACTION OF FEELINGS

If I were to paint now,
I would paint
A triangular shape:
One that would pirouette,
Curve and disappear
Onto a thin, vertical line
Perpendicular to the Earth:
Like a whippoorwill
Atop a tall thin wire.

1982

INTEGRITY

Fate has finally stripped her clean,
To stand as pure in the open sky
As a winter star. Fate is it?
Or is the continuous Self
So strong as to cause this isolation?

Did the need to be in touch
With the universe again,
That heavenly state before being,
Come forth so strongly in her
That she has become juxtaposed in space
To settle a restless self?

Was it the need to cease
Sweating it out that made her stop;
Like those still moments beside the road
When she would stare into
Freely moving creeks
To feel the current of herself
Only to be pulled away by duties calling?

Fate has finally freed her
From meaningless tasks,
Or has she freed herself
By stopping the living lie?

1983

THE SUNROOM

Her eyes blur from too many
Sun-blanched walls;
Her blood runs like paste,
Everything tastes the same.

Her only feeling is the heavy
Throb that keeps her here;
Only the dogs at her feet
Perk their ears to hear
Each sound the day makes.

A few slow bumblebees
Climb the outside walls;
Heavy heaps of snow
Melt into mud.

She waits for that seed of energy
To plant itself again in her,
And grow full and green
As it had been.

1983

COMPATIBILITY

Is to be completely oneself
In another's company;
Being with people and things
We are comfortable with.

Almost everything is
Incompatible with me these days:
Cigarette smoke, car fumes,
Droning noises, standing in line,
People who always complain...

I want to shake loose
And dance on the water
Like sunlight,
Completely myself,
Where time is space for joy.

1986

MIND SPACE

As far as mind's blue eye can see,
A lighthouse stands at the helm
Of a weathered, clapboard village;
Where pink roses sleep on picket fences,
And white sails gently bob and clang
Above brightly-colored vessels;
Where the narrow, shingled streets
Are lined with precious shops
And cozy little eateries.

1984

BURIED IN PHILADELPHIA

No one cried the day my brother died;
Only a very few,
Except for his lover,
Even knew he was slipping away.

Months before it was apparent
That Fate had taken hold on him;
The grieving started then, for us,
But no one cried the day he died.

Mother said he stopped by whole
In her dream the night before
And said goodbye...
That we'd have a service when
His ashes arrived from New York;
It would be very private,
Only a very few.

The service was graveside:
A tiny wooden box sat square on Astroturf;
A grand canopy covered a tiny crowd;
Stiff upper lips
Collapsed from time to time.

I knew my brother would
Have wanted to be buried here,
Here, on the main line, between
Grandfather and Uncle Penn—
A college president at thirty-five.

continued

His lover told me on the train
Going back to New York City,
That my brother really didn't give a damn
About being buried on the main line;
And did I know he had wanted to be
A minister at one time?

1986

DRIVING HOME

She notices, how like
An orange and purple scarf
The cool silk night descends;
How the mountain's
Dark mink coat
Cozies little lamp-lit homes
Lying nestled, scattered,
Like pieces of a rhinestone necklace
Dropped from granddame's throat.

She notices, how
The road is turning slate grey now;
She stays close to the center line,
'Til she gets back to where all hope
Shatters like a crystal glass
Emptied of a vintage wine.

1989

CLEAR WINDOWS

Moments of keen clarity,
Come like looking
At what we know
Through newly polished glass:

Moonlight is brighter
On the snow,
Stars are whiter
Through the evergreens,
And the soft smoke
Curling in the sky
Reminds us we are Home.

1989

OMEN: A STATE OF MIND

That symbol of fear,
Appeared as mysteriously
As a black cat on a dead tree;
Until the red collar
Around his neck,
Revealed his gentle domesticity.

1989

WARNING

Red embers light thin clouds
This pale, cold, coral morn;
Charred silhouettes of barren trees
Stand before a world asleep,
Unaware the birds are gone.

Deep the chill in bones of those
Who warned a wanton world,
To stand prayer-still,
In thought and awe,
To prepare a hopeful Dawn.

1990

TOUCH OF THE DOVE

What soft feathers touch my head
And on my shoulders rest?
What Light surrounds me
And reveals that what we see
Is Mystery dressed so brilliantly?

Why are the shining silver creeks,
The great green rocks and trees,
The mud and moss of pine-fast cliffs,
Now, so bright to eye and ear
And dear to feel beneath my feet?

What is this Peace that captures mind
In thought, where water falls?
What is this boundless rainbow joy
That breaks black clouds
Of fear and dread?

Is it the manifest of Holy Love,
The presence of the Dove, we feel?
Who comes to disenthrall us
From blindness, and cause us see
The world we tread, and hold it dear?

1991

TEMPLE EVERGREEN

When I walk into this house
In the woods,
After a heated, frantic time;
I seem to sink down deep
Into the smooth, cool earth;
Down through rich blues
And evergreens,
Becoming one with Light;
And in my wide soft easy chair,
I listen, sparkle, and
Drink pure water for a while.

From this sacred place,
Birds sound sweeter, sharper;
Deer move silently
As falling snow.
Now, I see a crow
Sweep through the trees;
While I emerge
Like a simple woodchuck
From his winter sleep.

1991

REDEMPTION

When what we see on Earth
Becomes Divine,
Gloriously transformed
By radiant Light;
When the golden sun
Shines forth
From the deep black night;
And all Creation
Shivers bright with joy
At the warming touch
Of all-pervading Peace,
All-redeeming Love;
Will You then appear
In splendor
As promised by the rainbow
And a jet-stream cross?

1991

INTIMATE JOURNEY

Close to Thee at night,
Close as rain to earth,
Deep as dark
As ocean's depth
We touch to reach
Exquisite Light;
Returning to
A place pre-birth,
Of all-pervading
Love and Peace.

1991

ETERNAL LIFE

There comes
A deep release of self
When we embrace
The wind, the earth;
When we listen
To the ancient trees,
Calm hills,
The pounding
Pouring seas,
Shining creeks
And skies.

They fill us with
An all-pervading peace
Of a loving universe;
A place pre-birth,
Where we become
One with all that was
And is, and will be
Through eternity.

1991

BEAUTY

Beauty
Is a state of grace,
A quality quite never lost;
The Perfect
In the imperfect;
The Unseen,
Face to face;
The presence of Divine
In ordinary things.

Beauty
Is Light
Shining
Through a crystal frost,
Making lace
Of meadow grass,
And palaces
For homeless kings.

1991

FROM THE GREENHOUSE

Don't linger too long in solitary thought,
Lest you fall from the bough
That brought you to this magic height;
For while you wait and watch
For that priestly-vested Soul in white
To take you home,
The Sun comes in to take away the night,
And leaves you shining
In a chartreuse dome of golden Light,
A sparkling place
To run and dance and sing.

1991

CELESTIAL DAY

The fields are glazed an icing white
This happy birthday morn;
Tall crystal candles are alight
Atop a chocolate mountain cake;
Pine green boughs
Their powdered sugar shake;
Oh, that I might have a bite
Of this celebrated Earth, transformed!

1991

VOLUPTUOUS

The creek is black at night,
Flowing rich and slick
As oil reflecting light;
Shining wet as a
Winding snake;
Moving like a woman,
In a sleek black slip,
Inside a moon-lit room.

1992

THE ORANGE GARDEN

Clap hands for the juggler;
Clap hands for the dolphin;
How sweet the koala;
How sweet the baby.
Clap for joy,
Hug for joy;
Coo and kiss
Their dear sweet cheeks,
Their innocence,
The pure sweet pleasure
Of their company,
While there is still
Time to smell the
Fragrance of the blossoms
And the sweet, sweet scent
Of dusk's calm air.

Clap hands for the
Bright red bird;
Clap, dance, and sing
Adoringly;
Praise the Earth;
Praise the Heavens;
Praise the Animals;
Praise the Humans;
Praise the Cause
Of all these things.
Let the sun set orange
Upon the land;
Let the moon
Rise white upon the sea.

1992

SING PRAISES

When morning breaks
The Silence of the woods;
As night recedes,
Dark trees come forward,
Brighter, Greener
From the deep;
On branch and nest,
Tiny feathered breasts
And throats
Emote such song,
So rich, so variegated, sweet,
That all awake
To join the pitch and beat
That celebrates a luminous dawn.

Red wing, blue,
Sweep down, soar through
The canopy of hemlock,
Oak and pine;
Sing praises
To the Presence of Divine
In all that lives
By water, air and light.

Red deer, cricket, turtle, snake
Go about your day
In thicket, marsh and rock.
Brook-trout, bee,
Earthworm and wasp,
Move along in your delight;

continued

71

Let human hands and feet
Beware your right
To come and go
As God sees fit.

1992

HOLY WATER

I love the Rain,
The healing sound of it
Dripping wet,
Tapping leaves,
Sheeting down
On blowing trees,
Stirring Earth;
Crashing down
And over cliffs,
Pounding like sea;
Rushing over creek bed
Stones and grass;
Splashing me,
Bringing rebirth.

I love the Rain,
The healing touch of it
Anointing me;
Cascading down
Inside the cavern
Of my head

Into my bones;
Flowing deep,
Filling my veins,
Making me whole,
Keeping me pure,
Ending still
And round as moon,
Reflecting Soul.

continued

I love the Rain,
The healing smell of it
Releasing cedar incense
From the ground,
Blessing me.

1992

SYMPHONY OF CREATION

When night's calm curtain
Lifts away the Moon,
Before the Maestro
Taps his stick
To bring Creation
Into Daylight's song;
One by one,
The animals, plants and rocks
Prepare to join in one
Sweet sylvan symphony;
Become one grand harmonic hall
Of all that lives
By water, air and light.

1992

THE RIVER

As morning tips green trees in gold,
Making brilliant, chartreuse gems
Of lucent leaves;
Beyond the woods
A mud-green river flows,
And dazzles wide,
Like a sheet
Of winding liquid glass
That swans glide on by day;
And by the luminous eve,
Cools to a mirror still
And silver smooth,
Reflecting blue and coral light.

1992

FOR CREATION'S HEALING

Peace and healing be to you,
Raccoon, high in the tree,
Bandit of the woods;
Peace and healing be to you,
Crow, so full of flesh and argument;
Peace and healing be to you,
Red bird and blue;
To you, sweet fawn and sapling tree,
Peace and healing be;
Peace and healing be to you,
Creek, mottled fish, frog and rock;
Peace and healing be to you,
Fretful child at mother's knee;
Biting, pinching hand and arm;
Peace and healing be to you,
Prisoner of discontent;
May God's bright Light and Grace,
Love, Peace, Hope and Joy,
Fill you and me,
And all that lives, forevermore.

1993

ONE

When I am broken with my life
And want to leave this world,
I get into my car
And drive too fast
On roads that wind with creeks
All lined with evergreens
Who lift me up:
Wind, Earth, Sky, and I
Become one
By the Spirit who dwells in me,
Makes me whole
And leads me on.

1993

LIGHTDANCE

Moving patch of chartreuse light,
Bright-green gem, cause of my delight!
All the day is yours to dance and play
From dawn to noon to early night;
May I be like you 'til clouds bring rain;
Then, become a cool and crystal drop,
'Til I can be like you again,
Playing hide-and-seek in Paradise.

1993

TRANSFORMATION

Life on Earth in the Spirit
Life on Earth in the Presence,
Life on Earth in the mind of God,
Life on Earth in the Word;
Earth transformed by the Light.
Thy Kingdom come,
Thy will be done
In all the Universe
As it is in Heaven.
Our Source, who art in all that is,
Hallowed be thy names.

1993

SOURCE

Spirit, let my life reflect You
Like a sun-filled waterfall;
My soul reflect You like
A pond around the moon.

Let my Spirit glisten
Like spring grass,
And my heart burst forth
Like blossoms on the trees,
By Your indwelling.

Move within me as a
Cold clear creek moves
Down through pine-fast woods;
Be my well-spring
Today and always.

1993

QUALIFY A BROKEN HEART

A loss of love so deep,
The heart is pressed
And twist and wrung
'Til every drop of blood and tear
Is spent on what is gone.

Unfathomed grief,
The heart wrenched forth
And flung into a hole so dark,
No star is there, no break of light,
No hope, no God-relief.

Until a flooding calm
Brings peace and wide release;
What paradox
The rushing in of Life again,
To make the human whole.

1994

DIVINE ENCOUNTER

While walking on a path
Out to the creek's far point,
Where she meets the sound,
I met a figure
In the morning mist
Who appeared to me
While I was deep in thought,
Looking at the ground.

I had been wishing, for so long,
To know who God is
And would I be OK?
And then the answer came:
A Love so unconditional,
So profound,
Flooded up in me,
Burst open my heart;
But as I turned around,
The figure in the mist
Had gone away.

I knew then,
That nothing I would ever do
Could separate
That Love from me.
My wish was granted;
I was freed
From the angst of what
I had so feared.

1997

ILLUMINE

Soaked by Your Presence,
Bathed by Your Grace,
Soaked, saturated, full
To overflowing with You;
Oneness with You, peace.
All that heightens my sense
Of You—the music, nature,
Laughter, love and light—
Makes a stain-glassed
Window of my life;
Paradise is here with You!

1997

STUCK

Not giving enough,
Giving too much;
Spending days and nights
With an old black dog
Who lights her life;
Wearing down gray
Sidewalks to the shops;
Buying larger clothes
With no real place to go;
Spending much on gifts
And not enough
To mend the world,
Waiting for Friday night
'Til the one she loves comes;
Sleeps in all day Saturday,
Then goes back Sunday noon
And she can only feel relief.

1999

TO A TISSUE

Through the years
Women have found
That tears, not diamonds,
Are their best friends.
Tears of laughter, grief
And joy profound,
Anger sentiment and rage,
Flood their eyes to
Bring relief and peace;
And help them face
Oncoming age,
Blind-siding change.

2001

FLIGHT

Without the weight
Of organs, muscles, bones,
I am free, I am air,
Flowing like clear water
Down through huge gray stones
Into a blue-green cavern,
So deep, so high, that there,
I can fly and soar as eagles do
Through Heaven's door.

2002

REMEMBERING

Laughter's echo,
Brings memories
Of a childhood gone;
Calls me home
Like a mothers voice,
A moonlit path,
A ship's bell
Ringing from
Very far away.

2002

INCARNATE

Fair portal to Reality unseen,
You embody fullness of it,
Sacre Coeur.
As the soft white Dove
Mortals covet
In their blackest dream;
You are the brightest light,
Within, beside, below, above us,
Healing the fear
That will bruise and mark us
When our way
Is darkest and unclear.
The way that saves us,
You approve of, is love.
Dearest One,
You are Love,
Love-in-action seen.

2004

SILVER LIGHT

Sometimes, when the cove is overcast,
The sun looks like a light bulb
Shining through smoked glass.
Though brighter than the moon,
The sun takes on the coolness of her,
Doesn't dominate the day.
Rather, speaks in silent shimmer,
While staying undercover,
Seeming oh, so far away.

2004

THE GRAVE YARD IN MARCH

Two gray gulls perch on the bough
Of a downed gray birch;
While I sit still in my cold gray car,
Looking out at cold gray hills,
Gray sky, gray clapboard homes
Along the cove, all in different tones;
And then, I think of the gray bones
That must lie under me;
Suddenly, I am glad
That my blood is red and warm;
That I'm alive.

2004

HEROES

Wind, walloping down the cove,
Whipping worn-out U.S. flags
Secured on graveyard stones
Set in chartreuse grass;
While in a wind most cutting cold,
I am warm, lit by a Love so deep,
It burns a hollow in my heart
For Joy to fill; a Joy that will,
One day, I hope, be bold,
Spring forth to wet dry ground.

I wonder how those soldiers died,
Were they brave or crazed?
Why is a hero not one who boldly lives,
But one who's almost always dead?
Are not those whose ways are kind,
In a wanton world gone mad,
The true heroes: those who live
To "remove the occasion for all war,"
As George Fox, a pacifist, once said?

2004

FOG

Ducks swim in the mist,
Like shadow figures on a wall;
Standing on sharp rocks,
They poke their feathers clean.
The waking folk in town
Bathe in the mist
Of their tiled showers;
I could reflect on fog for hours,
But it is too temporary.

2004

RETURNING

Jumping out of the comfort zone
Here, full, where once I empty came;
I leap toward the comfort of fond faces
And arms of friends I left behind;
Look to new experiences in old places;
Find and be myself again
In spaces You and I create.

Funny, how that little waterfall
And creek that I once knew,
Now listens best, has time for me,
When all the rest are other-pressed.

2004

ON THIN ICE

She crawls on crystal sheets of glass so thin,
She fears that when they shatter,
She will fall into that dark abyss
Where only a lover's kiss,
With arms to embrace her
Could save her;
Tell her that she somehow matters;
Or until a good friend calls.

2004

ABIDING

I just want to sit by flowing creeks
And blowing trees,
Where I can steep awhile
And breathe;
Let go of ego and just be.
That's Heaven on Earth for me,
Deep listening, hearing Thee.

2004

AUTUMN

Stopping by a creek
To listen to her flow;
Cars rush by, drown her out
And yet, I do not go.
I want to hear the trees
Along her creek bed breathe:
Exhale red, orange, brown,
Gold and yellow leaves.

2004

DYING TO LIVE

Bury my bones beneath the ground,
That I may rot and merge with Earth;
For only in her womb
Have I been whole,
Known beauty, health,
Silence, and joy profound.

From birth, I've known her as my home.
Without tent, burrow, or casket now,
I'll rest in peace;
For in her, I am sound and safe,
My spirit freed.

So, if I wonder off to die, worry not;
For I am drawn to holy spaces,
Places where I can simply be
With the One whose life
Has been a crystal creek
Flowing up in me,
To make my face
Shine like gold
Through autumn leaves.

2004

PINE TREES

Why do green majestic pines,
That I, from kitchen window, see;
Bring me to such soaring heights,
As they catch morn and evening light?
Trees are simply leased to us,
To instill joy, bring rest, deep peace.

2005

WINTER RIDE

How thrilling to ride the open road,
In chilling cold,
Along curving, pine-fast cliffs;
Where snow, like icing, drips
Down stacked, shattered rocks;
And white birch trees
Bend into the sun.
It is as if I blend in with these,
My stalwart, winter friends.

2005

TURQUOISE DREAM

That I could be by mountain creek,
Flowing full and pure of melting snow;
Be by surrounding mesas
Full of golden morning light;
As they turn to pink and purple
Then disappear into a black-starred night.
But, if by them I cannot be,
May they go where I go, reside in me.

2005

MOVING ON

Wanting to be left alone,
With just one word, one move;
As if with silver-handled knife,
She swiftly sliced me from her life,
Kept the slicing smooth;
Cut me deeply, to the bone.
When will the bleeding stop?
How long can torment last?
When I gain clarity, move on,
Then forgive what's passed?

2005

TO A CREEK

Splashing over stones,
Like laughter after pain;
Flowing like a diva
In green satin gown with train;
I hold my eyes on you
And celebrate
Your joy from this spring rain,
Of gentle, steady drops
That cause shiny leaves to bend
And mottled frogs to hop
In a pond nearby street's end.

Standing here on creek bed ground,
I see pools of rain so green,
I only know them from the trees
By sound and shine and sheen.

2005

NEWPORT

The place
Where wide water
Meets the docks,
And yachts as large
As ships park there;
Where tourists
Gather round
White plastic chairs
To hear the band
At four o'clock;
The place
To dance,
Drink wine
And chat,
Savor seafood,
Succulent and sweet;
The place
Where orange sunsets
Flood the clouds…
So striking this,
I fall in love again
With the One above
And the one I'm with.

2005

TO THE WIND

You make white wicker chairs
To rock and doors to slam;
Sea grass to speak,
White caps to churn,
Gulls to dip and soar.
You stir poems in us
That, like debris,
Wash up on shore
After a storm;
Seekers find them
In wet sand,
Treasure in their hands
And repeatedly adore.

2005

CHURCH AT THE BEACH

The summer Sunday service,
In the morning, on the beach
Is outdoor church
Where worship ought to be:

For those who won't
Wear dressy clothes
Or sit in hard, dark pews;
Who choose to sit in circle,
In awe, on cloth, in sand;
Sing hymns, and pass the
Sacrament of bread and
Wine by hand.

How like that first small band
Who flocked to Jesus by the sea,
As he healed the sick
And preached good news
To those at Galilee.

2005

PARADISE WITHIN

Enter through the door of Silence,
Paradise within.
Go deep, Breathe;
Inhale the fragrance
Of the garden there as Peace.
Exhale the fragrance through
Your heart as Love;
Let all that blocks the Spirit's
Flow within you, cease.
Be Grace and Goodness
Gushing up in you.
Be a font to all you meet.
Fly with the Eagle and the Dove;
Give, Receive.
Paradise unfolds through you.

2005

THE HEALING CHAPEL

She sits before an altar lit
By candle and stained glass;
She hears the lilting song
Of little birds outside,
Hopping on green grass.
Here, inside these
Stone sanctuary walls,
She is touched by Grace,
Who rights all wrongs,
Opens up her heart,
Lights her face,
And calls her
To unhindered life.

2005

MOTHER'S HUSBAND

In the waterfall she hears his laughter;
In the bluest sky she sees
The sparkle of his caring eyes.
She remembers him as tall, lean,
Calm and strong,
Handsome, kind, humor keen.
He was a farm-bred boy,
A Navy man with a Purple Heart,
Loving God, of modest means.
His family, pets and friends
Meant most to him.

But he most adored his second wife.
He cared for her as if she were
Made of porcelain and silk;
Yet, he couldn't break her as he held her
And hugged her warm and tight.
Their life was like the cream of milk;
Their love, like morning light.

Then, dementia slowly stole him from her;
Stole the sparkle and laughter of their years;
Left him silent with a vacant stare.
As she became the one to care,
She turned from silk to cotton,
Porcelain to stone.
Her loss was almost more
Than she could bear.

continued

109

In a nursing home,
He finally turned to skin and bone
And died, alone, but not forgotten;
For she was there in heart, in mind and tears.

His journey home to Bliss was bright
And swift as shooting stars.
In the photographs, music and the wine,
She keeps their precious times alive;
The memory of one so dear loving her,
Is her heaven here.
Though feeling left behind,
She sometimes feels, in a gentle breeze,
The blessing of his kiss.

2006

GENEROSITY

Let me tell you about two
Most kind to me;
When I was lonely
Without, what seemed,
A caring friend;
Both were strangers
Who included me,
Brought me into humanity,
Accepted me as I am.

They manifested God to me:
One was slow, the other poor.
The first gave me a smile
So genuine, real, divine;
The other a penny when,
As a child, I needed one;
I had four and needed five.

Their generosity reminds me
Of the time a Light
So brilliant shined:
I saw an old man sleeping
On a worn-out bench outside,
So vulnerable to crime.

I offered him twenty dollars;
He, at first, declined
(He seemed so dignified);
Then, as I walked away,
Out he cried with, "Yes"

continued

111

And, "May Gold Bless."
Then, above us, in the sky,
A bright Light flashed around us.
To eternity, it seemed to bind us.

2006

LOVED

On my grandmother's doorstep,
As a child, I remember,
That before I went inside,
A wide Light embraced me;
I felt loved and recognized.

2006

HEAVEN ON EARTH

Maybe Heaven's not for me,
Though I would enjoy the buoyancy!
Here in the body's density,
I feel pain and sorrow,
Fear tomorrow;
But here, at least,
I can taste the feast
Of all that is;
Touch skin and fur;
Hear chirp and purr;
Kiss and touch
And see what is so dear to me.
If Heaven were on Earth and
All our senses tuned to Bliss,
I would welcome wholeness, joy
And stay transfigured,
Resurrected here.

2006

DIRECTION

Pain brought her to her knees
When she was on a path
She was pleased to be on.
Something inside her
Was not, as yet, released;
God had plans to free her.

2006

SPRING

Shekinah:
These translucent blades
Of bright green grass,
That rise up tender,
Gleam and glisten,
Among dead dry leaves
Of winter past;
While waterfall,
Sun-sheened and clean
After a heavy rain,
Drops rushing down
A bursting creek
To run through her again.

Stepping over stones
By bank of
Newly budding trees.
She thinks how much she loves
The chilly warmth
This chartreuse season brings.

2006

AWAKENING

That discordant chord of bird song,
Through rays of morning mist;
Shifts the listening soul
To sounds of earthly bliss.

2006

PONDERING

In nineteen-ninety,
What force pulled her off the road
To listen to the Earth;
To put aside her own agenda,
Experience a rebirth;
Know intimacy with Spirit,
Explore Creation's worth?

2006

CHAPEL IN THE WOODS

I remember how in our woods,
After a storm in nineteen ninety-one,
A large limb broke off one tree,
Was flung into the crux of another one,
Forming an awesome cross
That everyone could see.

A dream came later on that spring:
I was sitting on a stump beneath that tree
Wearing a long green dress,
Holding, between my knees,
A large wooden bowl
That held two loaves of bread.
Why does that memory haunt me now,
Insisting to be writ and read?

2006

MOON AT FOSTER COVE

Moon must have dropped her necklace
On the quiet cove last night;
Because I saw gold shimmer
As the tide came in with morning light,
Under silver seagull wings.

Marsh, splendid in her own green gown,
Wears moon's gold necklace now.
But moon has many more to share,
Bright tiaras of sparkling stars,
For maiden planets fair to wear.

This eve, she'll wake, mid pink bouquets,
From sleek, blue satin sheets;
Rise high to rule the sky;
Make silver linings for her king
Who slips away, all done with day.

2007

WIND PEOPLE

Wind people,
Are people moved by wind;
Like sails that wait
For wind to blow.

Wind people know
That wind is Spirit
Deep Within;
And round about
Outside of them.

Wind people co-create,
Extend their Source;
Are God's intention,
Made manifest,
In the expanding universe;
Are different
From the rest;
Stir up things
As they go by.

Rock people,
Stay put like trees,
Bear storms and cold.

Fire people,
Set aflame
All within their path,
Their passions stirred,
Intentions bold.

continued

Water people,
Quench the fire
In those who thirst;

She can be all of these
At different times.
Who is she?
One who fully lives
And fully loves,
So full of God;
Christ, her rudder here.

2007

NEW ENGLAND WINTER

Underneath bright ice
My free creek flows,
Through frozen layered rocks
And limbs bent down
With heavy snow;
She flows down beneath
A covered bridge,
A rushing waterfall,
To a glen of weathered trees;
To far beyond
Where I can barely see;
Yet, I know she shimmers on.
From where I stand
At the red barn door,
I have seen her come to rest
Under the frozen pond,
Waiting there for ice to thaw.

2007

IN STILLNESS WE ARE ONE

In Stillness, when I have no thought,
The woods and I are truly one;
Frost-laced leaves on bright white snow,
Bare, brittle, icy boughs above,
Landscape the inner side of me.

The furry body by my side
Reminds me I am not alone
When I am deeply steeped in Thee.
So bound together by Your Love,
Are we one or two or three?

2008

CHURCH OUTDOORS

In deep woods with stalwart pines
I feel alive and energized;
Although a chill sets in my bones,
I feel so whiskey warm inside,
Lit, as if, by red coal fire.

Awaiting heavy, silent snow,
I huddle under blankets warm,
Feeling safe in this still peace;
Embraced by Love so great, so wide
I feel no longer spent and torn;

My true church, the wide outdoors!
My poetry, my prayerful song.
My life, God's gift of love to me;
My life in Christ, forever free!
My joy is here with stalwart trees.

2008

RED BIRD NOW

Red bird, bright on blackened bough
Why do you come to cheer me now?
I alone so full of fright,
Lifted by your brilliant sight,
Wonder how my God could know
How bleak my world appeared last night.

2012

GOD HAS FAVORITES

So wanting to be the light
Of someone's eye,
Realizing the longing of
Her heart, she wept;
Knowing no one
Would hear her cry but God;
Knowing God has favorites.

2012

BALCONIES

Sit with me love of mine;
Let our hearts entwine
Like citrus vines,
Make juicy climb
Up mango tree,
To waste ourselves
In sunlit breeze,
Dance on blue water,
Ever free!

2012

PART III.

FRIENDS' ANSWERED PRAYER STORIES

A Young Mother's Story

We had two great kids, and now with another one on the way, I was excited—been there, done that. Soon came the day of C-section number three. My husband and I anxiously waited in the room for the doctors to be ready. We felt good. When the personnel came in, however, all of a sudden our comfort zone started to crumble and we got a dose of Connecticut versus Utah hospital birthing policies. In Utah, the rooms were brightly colored and cheery. My husband had been encouraged to be with me from beginning to end: holding my hand, talking me through what he was observing, and sharing his fascination and thrill as he watched our first two children being born.

In Connecticut, he wouldn't be allowed in the room for my prep, and during surgery he had to stay behind a curtain and wouldn't be allowed to observe. The "dad-to-be" disappointment was obvious. The helpful, friendly attitudes of previous doctors and nurses were replaced with more calloused, business-like curtness. I gave a half-hearted smile as they wheeled me away to the operating room. Without talking, the anesthesiologist administered the epidural block, told me not to move, and then walked out.

Dressed in only a hospital robe, I started to shiver. The walls were dismal green. The lights were low and the room felt dark. I felt soooo alone and started to be frightened. I

131

could feel myself starting to get stressed, and since I was having this baby early because of high blood pressure, this was going to be a problem.

Anxious, I started to pray. I closed my eyes and very earnestly asked for help and assurance. Almost immediately, a beautiful portrait of Christ that hung in my living room came into my mind and the thought, "Don't worry—you aren't alone." I don't know how long I prayed, but the more I focused and talked with my Heavenly Father, the warmer and calmer I became. It was if He had wrapped a big comforter around me and snuggled me in, and I knew I wasn't alone. All of the panic subsided, and I was OK. I am grateful for assurance that continues to come daily as I humbly pray, express gratitude for life, and ask for help. The knowledge that I am not alone still calms me—and I am OK.

Breath of God

One evening as I was on my way out of the hospital, a doctor stopped me with a request to visit one of his patients. She was a woman in her late 30s who had a long history of lung disease. According to the doctor, a large portion of one lung had been removed, and she was scheduled to have surgery the next morning to remove more. Her other lung was also not healthy. After each surgery she had less and less breathing capacity. The doctor was very worried about her and confided in me that there was little else he could do for her.

Eventually, there would not be enough of her lung left to remove more as her disease kept spreading. At that time the patient would die, and she was well aware of the situation. The doctor had just left her room. The patient had pulled down all of the shades in an otherwise bright room, turned off the lights, and was refusing to talk to anyone. Deep depression had set in. "She may not let you in or talk to you, but please try," were the doctor's parting words to me.

I approached her room, hoping that the patient would at least let me in to see her. As I opened the door, there was silence. I started by identifying myself and asked her permission to come in ... more silence. I sat in the chair next to her bed and hoped for some sign of recognition. Finally I broke one of the cardinal rules of chaplaincy: I started telling her about my own lung problems, which were multiple and all in the past. She turned toward me and started to listen. I wanted to talk about *her,* not me, so I said just enough to let her know that I was aware of some of what she was thinking and feeling.

As she perked up, she started asking me questions about my lung experiences. We finally left the subject of my lungs and talked only about her current situation. My history had made our connection possible when it seemed that she would never open up to anyone. After about 40 minutes, she agreed that it would be all right if I prayed for her. As I left, I did feel that she was a little better, but surgery the next morning was still ahead of her.

I was not in the hospital the next day. The following day I could not find her name on the patient list. I was very concerned that she had not made it through the surgery, and I was very sad. I went to talk to the nurses on her floor in search of some information. I was told that she went home. I asked why and was told that she did not have the surgery.

Later in the day, the doctor came up to me in the hall. "What did you do?" he inquired. When the doctor went into see her in the early morning before the surgery, he discovered that her lung was fine. She was breathing on her own and required NO SURGERY. He then sent her home.

In response to his question, I said, "I did nothing. We prayed for God's help and care."

A Missionary Story

My husband and I had served for three years in Brazil as missionaries and were preparing to return to the United States. I had not been feeling well and needed to have surgery but delayed doing it until our return. Upon my return, I visited my doctors and discovered that I really needed three procedures from two different doctors. I prevailed upon them to do all that was needed at the same time so I would not have to have two or three different surgeries. I became quite nervous as I was on the stretcher in the pre-op waiting room and knew that was not going to help me in a positive way, so I started praying for inner strength for me and for my doctors to use their best medical judgment.

I was pushed into the hallway, outside of the OR room, and I was in front of a large window that looked out onto a most beautiful mountain scene. I could feel my body begin to relax and gratitude filled my heart for my many blessings and for the beautiful creations of our Heavenly Father. I had not been given any medication at that point, but I relaxed enough that I went to sleep.

I went so deep in my sleep that I did not realize when they took me into the OR room, moved me from the stretcher onto the operating room table, started my anesthesia, did my surgery, finished my surgery, pushed me to the recovery room and in fact don't remember responding to them sufficiently to be moved back to my room several hours later. I do remember opening my eyes at one point and seeing someone standing near me with a red and white blouse, but remember nothing until I woke up at 10:00 A.M. the next morning— over 24 hours later. My father was at my bedside and commented, "Wow, I wondered if you would ever wake up."

I feel that my prayers for peace and confidence to get through the surgery were answered, and the tender mercies that I received throughout this ordeal were God's way of telling me that He accepted my efforts in serving Him in the Mission Field for three years.

A Teenager's Story

I get scared easily, especially after seeing scary movies. I replay the scary stuff over and over in my mind until I am actually afraid for my safety. This has lasted for years, and even while serving as a missionary, it can be hard to fall asleep at night. But half way through my mission I began to realize the significance of prayer; that we are God's children and are able to ask Him for what we need, no matter how big or small. Just as a parent cares about the small concerns of his or her child, God cares about what we care about; if it's important to us, it's important to Him.

So one evening, I was trying to sleep but was overcome with fear. It gripped my heart and my mind and I was on the verge of turning on the light and crying myself to sleep when the thought came to my mind that I should pray. I immediately clasped my hands together and said, "Heavenly Father, I'm scared and I need your help." Nothing happened; I still felt scared. Then the thought came to ask a question: "Heavenly Father, do I really need to worry about this?" With that question, a flood of peace flowed into my head and my heart and I knew that I was being watched over and that I had no need to fear.

The phrase from Genesis came to my mind, that though the serpent may bruise my heel, God has given man power to crush his head. And I knew that although scary things can happen to us and hard things may make moments tough, if we will turn to the Lord, then through the power of Jesus Christ we can overpower and overcome those trials.

I have been so grateful for that experience. Many nights the fear has returned and I have been able to pray and ask the Father to be with me and the peace has returned. I know that our Father in Heaven loves us and cares about us and is only a prayer away.

God Is My Shepherd

I was a chaplain in training at a major medical center. This experience happened early on in the year, and I was still pretty "green." I was the new kid on the block, and believe me, I felt just like that. From day one when I got my ID photo badge and a tour of the facility to the day when this happened, I felt like a duck out of water. I was wondering exactly why my rector had recommended this program as good training for me. I was interested in doing pastoral care in my local parish, but I felt totally unprepared for this hospital work. Bottom line: I was asking, "Why am I here, God?"

While waiting for the team of doctors to leave the patient I was planning to visit, I leaned against the wall and was contemplating: "Am I off in the wrong direction, or is this truly God's plan for me?"

As I looked into the room directly opposite from the person I was supposed to visit, I could see a small, lonely person all covered except from the nose up. The patient looked so sad that I decided to pop in and pay a visit while I was waiting.

She was a middle-aged woman who was very pleasant but scared to death of being in the hospital. She told me of the tests she was facing and the fear she had about the diagnosis. We chatted for a bit, and I asked her if it would be OK if I said a prayer for her. Her head nodded in the affirmative.

Placing my hand on her shoulder, I began praying. For the first time in my bedside prayers, I used the image of God as the shepherd caring for all of his flock. As I ended my prayer, I saw a tear start to roll down her cheek. I was afraid I had said something to upset her when my goal was to comfort her.

As she looked up at me with two wet eyes and a grin from ear to ear, she said; "How did you know that I am a shepherd? I have 64 sheep."

As I left her room, I said a little prayer of my own: "OK, God, thank you for sending the Holy Spirit to speak through me and for letting me know that this *is* where I belong."

PART IV.

METERED POEMS/HYMN TEXTS

Poems for Adaptation as
Hymn Texts
for the
Wider Christian Church

© 2008

GOD'S PEACE WILL COME

God's peace will come; Yes, God's peace will come,
When the Light of Christ comes into our hearts;
When mercy and love and justice embrace
The dignity of the whole human race
And the dawn of Heaven shines from each face.

Freedom will come; Yes, freedom will come,
When the Light of Christ comes into our hearts;
When mercy, and love and justice embrace
The dignity of the whole human race
And the dawn of Heaven shines from each face.

2008

BURY ME IN THE
GREEN-BROWN EARTH

Bury me in the green-brown earth,
Stand round in mirth and jubilee;
Friends, mourn loss of my company,
But I shall be where I was birthed!

The sweet hope of the living God
Is in the sod and mustard seed;
Death, but a deep release of me
In Spirit to abide with Thee.

Hallelu, for the vineyard life
Because Christ died for you and me!
The sweet hope of the Trinity
Is Heaven on Earth and end of strife.

Bury me in the green-brown earth,
Stand round in mirth and jubilee;
I'm bound in Christ eternally,
Where I was birthed, there, I am free!

2008

THERE IS A FLAME
WITHIN HER SOUL

There is a flame within her soul
That boldly burns with passion bright;
A light that burns all day and night
And never flickers from her goal
To turn the wanton world round right.

A beacon to lost boats and ships
That float adrift upon the bay;
And never come to sandy shore
Afraid they might, in slips, just stay
Lined up along the busy coast.

Yet wanting so calm port in storm
And fire to keep them fully warm,
They sail nearby to keep the light
That from her clear bright beacon comes
To welcome them back home again.

2008

MY PEACE WILL
BE YOUR GROUNDING

When all around me is the fray
That hinders how I go or stay;
And the rise of pressure pounding
In my veins is so astounding,
I wait, hold very, very still.

In the deep down calm, I can feel
Jesus' loving arms around me,
Hear him to me console and say:
My sister [brother] all is well today!
My peace will be your grounding now.

2008

HOW LOVELY IT IS HERE

In early morn when I arise,
I know your Spirit's ev'rywhere;
Though clock in hall ticks out the time,
I am in timeless Paradise.

Here with You, true time stands still.
In this blissful, eternal Thou;
Help me discern to keep your will,
Cherish joy of Your sweet life now.

How long have we, Creation, known
That you, alone, fill all the Earth?
Your Spirit present ev'rywhere
Brought us from listless dust to birth.

You shower us with unbound Love
And lift our groaning by your Grace.
How lovely here when you appear
As peace, in all hearts, hands, and face.

2008

YOU ARE IN EVERYTHING

You are in the mountain morning light,
The wind that circles through the trees.
You are in the ocean, sky, and breeze,
And stars I see from bed at night.

You are in the crying newborn child,
The wrinkles of a poor man's face.
You are in the raging captive's cage,
The soulful eyes of Nature's wild.

You, the gracious Presence in our souls,
Make broken lives to dance and sing
With peace and joy only You can bring.
You are the Life that makes us whole.

You are the Love that rebinds our hearts,
The Wisdom of all simple ways.
You, the help and hope of all our days,
That gives us rise to make fresh starts.

Hallelu! Your being everywhere,
With us even through doubt and fear;
For always being so ever near,
Keeping us in Your loving care.

2008

BESIDE THE FLOWING STREAM

In stillness, Lord, I wait for you
Beside the gently flowing stream;
As spent deer pants for drink and rest,
I, too, long for life anew.

Let your Spirit flow through me
To be a font for all who need
Love, joy, hope and tenderness,
Wide release from fearing death.

Bless your creatures here on Earth,
May their sweet lives truly thrive;
Open hearts to Your life breath,
May your Spirit nourish us.

In stillness, Lord, I wait for you
Beside the gently flowing stream;
Water that I once ran by
Now does gently run through me.

2008

IN STILLNESS, LORD, I WAIT FOR YOU

Be still and know that I am God.
In stillness, Lord, I wait for You.
Let Your Light and Wisdom shine
Bright inside my sorry soul.

Be still and know that I am God.
In stillness, Lord, I wait for You.
You provide the Grace we need
To free and lead our sorry souls.

You dwell within that holy space,
The place inside, where I can't hide;
There we meet in waters deep,
I do not sleep but listen for

Your still small voice that I adore;
When it bids me to rise to speak
Your truth fills ev'ry open heart,
Keeps us turned right even more.

Be still and know that I am God.
In stillness, Lord, I wait for You.
Wash all my weighty cares away
Help me not fall or go astray.

Let Your sweet love flow free from me
To those who truly seek your peace;
Seek wide release from dread and grief,
Death, dishonor, disbelief.

continued

In stillness, Lord, I wait for You;
Wait for You in stillness time.
I am Yours and You are mine.
In Joy, we dwell in Paradise.

2008

WHEN I STEEP IN SILENCE DEEP

Wake early, lone, with morning cup,
I wait for Spirit to rise up,
Steep instead in Silence deep;
Keep from going back to sleep.

You fill me up with Light and Love,
Make day bright, as from above;
Blow away my doubts and fears,
So that I can serve more clear.

What is this mighty Song within?
Joy that makes worship begin,
Grace that takes away all sin,
Praise that welcomes your Grace in.

2008

HAVE YOU SEEN THE WOUNDS OF WAR?

Have you seen the wounds of war
Of sane soldiers nailed to sand;
Sacrificed for freedom's sake,
Staked in another land for mine?

Jesus, nailed by feet and hands,
Freely died for freedom too;
Freedom of an inward kind,
One liberating hearts and minds.

Have you seen the inner wounds
And sores of those scarred souls
Who are most distressed by war?
Those whom war makes sick, insane?

Why do most not understand
That hate and war must cease?
That inner, outer conflict
Cannot mirror love, joy, peace;

This creation, Jesus tried
To make whole before He died;
Now His Spirit still our Guide,
As it has been throughout time,

Begs us now to love each other;
End the horror of our crimes,
Now become His New Creation;
As lion lies beside the lamb.

2008

WHEN SUDDENLY
WE ARE HIT BY STORM

When, suddenly we are hit by storm
That in no way are we prepared
For the destruction, death of form
That shakes our very being scared;
The path of Nature takes her course,
We cannot make sense of her force.

Be still and know, hold fiercely fast
The root and rock of our new birth;
Forget the fallen, sordid past;
Shall last our solid Spirit worth,
Preserved well In God's sweet Heaven
By the life our Lord has given.

Listen, body, mind, heart soul!
What Love, not wrath, has kindly wrought
Will make us everlasting whole.
Loved ones in Heav'n tender our thought;
Nature, may we forgive her ways,
Her beauty, bounty sustains our days.

2008

WHEN THE LIGHTS GO OUT

When lights go out, I'm not afraid,
I feel Your presence ev'rywhere;
I dream of Heav'n, yet You are here
Beside, above, below, within.

You, true Light, love of my soul;
Stay with me all through the dark;
You, my Life, Your love consoles,
Make my heart now bear your mark.

When lights go on, I'm not afraid,
I feel Your presence ev'rywhere;
I dream of Heav'n, yet You are here
Beside, above, below, within.

2008

THE ONE WHO
SHARES OUR GRIEF

Where can we go to cry aloud
To let the crowds know all our pain?
Who hears those screams held deep inside
Shouting in our loaded brains?

The One who always shares our grief,
Yet often seems so far away,
Is right here, inside our strife,
Awaiting our return today.

2008

WHY SHOULD THEY SUFFER?

When the meat of a beaten cow
Becomes part of my evening meal;
I swallow all the shame I feel,
Bless God for my survival now.

Why should they suffer so inside?
They are Creation's family!
Why should a plant, too, die for me?
More so for me that Jesus died!

Life here for all is sacrifice;
Hear the moaning of a mother!
We need show respect for other,
For all Creation as a friend.

2008

FACETS OF A DIAMOND

Like the facets of a diamond,
Reflecting bright and royal light;
Set in radiant, sweet splendor,
We're all facets of the Christ.

We all sparkle in the sunlight
As if lit by fire within;
Facets dazzles bright like rainbows
When is gone the blot of sin!

Dear God of Heaven, God of Earth
May our image reflect Thine;
Rebind, now, our hearts in kindness,
We are wed to you, remind us!

2008

GOLDEN LIGHT, SHINE DIVINE

Golden Light, shine Divine
Upon this doleful face of mine;
Infuse me with Your golden Light,
So that I may shine more bright.

With glad face may I then be
Better image of You in me;
With open arms, may I embrace
Dear ones bent in deep disgrace.

May I be Your light to them,
To bring them out of life's mayhem;
To show them how to rest in Thee
From storms raging on their sea.

Show them how to become still
To center in Your loving will;
Find the way to be reborn,
N'er again so tossed and torn!

Your light in me, a fire warm,
To comfort those who in life's chill,
Need to know Your gentle grace,
That golden light upon my face.

2008

RESURRECTION DAY

When golden glint of spring's new light
Topples ripples in the creek;
Sunbeams warm and squinting bright
To winter-weary souls speak;

I face God in gratitude
For seasons of renewal;
For Nature's greenest plentitude,
Rain dropping em'rald jewels;

Diamonds dropping all around,
Dark brown earth to turn bright green;
Even birds make diff'rent sounds
When fair spring spreads out her sheen.

Buds shoot forth, soft pinks and whites;
Bulbs break open through the Earth;
New day comes in, gone dark night;
Resurrection day, new birth.

2008

YOUR WILL TO LOVE
IS MY COMMAND

When it hurts so bad inside
That I cannot a human trust;
And what I long for most
Becomes a sacred must;
Into Your loving arms I flee.

When they tell me that I must
Press on in faithful fortitude
To fulfill my certain destiny,
I know my destiny is now,
Making hymns of pious poetry.

Praise to You, my trusted Trinity!
In Your grace I stand, abide;
However hard alone may be,
Your will to love is my command.

Your life is at our deepest core,
Speaks loudly when we stray;
But I am pulled back to your way,
Today, always in prayer.

2008

CALL OF THE MORNING DOVE

The haunting coo of morning dove
Makes me at my core aware
We are bound in Spirit's love;
All Creation in our care.

That in God's image we must be
God's faithful stewards here;
Tend gardens, farms, and factories
As sacred ground, all creatures dear.

Have we forgotten that the Earth
Matters so to God that S/He
Became one with us at birth;
Bound us in Love eternally?

Let us remember Christ in us
Begs our rebirth in Spirit;
Bear gifts of loving kindness;
Call of the Dove, you hear it?

2008

MORNING MOON

Morning moon, sweet owl, whoo whoo,
Up in bare, tall, silent tree;
Leads chorus of awaking birds
Who lift sweet voices up to Thee.

Morning moon, sweet dove, coo coo,
Up in bare, tall, silent tree;
Joins choir of awaking birds
Who lift sweet voices up to Thee.

Morning moon, sweet Christ Jesu,
In deep silence beckons me;
To join song of waking Earth
Who lifts voices up to Thee.

2008

STAY LIGHT, MY HEART

Stay light, my heart, in this dark world.
Be bright where hope dims dying souls.
Have you caused war or genocide?
Should you bear heavy guilt inside
And weight of grief for those involved?

You, heart, are made for love, compassion,
Bringing relief, peace, stirring passion!
So keep your God-belief, stay well,
Share all you can, sad times dispel.
Stay free, stay light, be dawn, be bright.

2008

WIND BLOW THROUGH ME

Wind blow through me,
Grace flow through me
As I go downwind,
Downstream.

Follow the fray,
Bring Peace today.
Send my mind,
Heart, hands to aid
All who need
Touch of God's Spirit;
Silence has
Brought me so near It.

2008

MAKING ART HEALS THE SOUL

When what makes emotions rise,
Fries our blood, evokes our cries;
Focus on what Spirit says:
Start creating, making art!

Sculpture, painting, poems, plays,
Music, dance, expressive ways;
Making art gives shape to prayer,
Art connects us to God's grace.

God's great gift, creative life;
Through making art, we let go strife,
By way of brush and palette knife,
Art heals the soul to make us whole.

2008

SHARING FACE TO FACE

One soul sharing face to face
Does more for the human race
Than most our mail-in charities!
Face-to-face, Jesus we feed,
Feel our human hearts ope up.

Not just money in a cup,
But face-to-face, lone hearts touch,
When we love, in-person give,
Imaging how Jesus was,
How He wanted us to live.

Something happens when we care,
Our hearts lighten, days are fair;
Heaven's light shines ev'rywhere
When we share with just one soul,
Take a moment to console.

2008

THANK YOU, GOD, FOR TUFTS OF GRASS

Thank You, God, for tufts of grass,
Lovely rooms through which we pass;
Friendship, family, creeks, and trees;
Cures for sickness and disease.

Thank You, God, for melodies,
Stirring hearts with tender love;
Keep us close to Your sweet Dove;
We ask You to save us now.

From storms that wreck communities,
Leaving us so grieved, forlorn;
Wars that leave us torn, despaired;
Poverty, crimes everywhere.

Lead us from misguided ways;
Bring us round by Your dear grace;
Be our center nights and days;
End our fruitless, frantic race.

Help us stay so steeped in Thee,
We forget our selfish needs,
Put Your will above our own;
Fill our lives with loving deeds.

Our hope, Dove of love and peace,
Olive branch that brings release
From fear, contempt, and hopelessness.
May we seek Your holiness.

2008

ALL TRUE HYMNS TO GOD ARE FAIR

All true hymns to God are fair;
True hymns come from everywhere!
Hymns of pure simplicity
Flow from hearts so naturally.

Simple hymns, like simple prayers,
Wrenching without pompous airs,
Praising without pomp that blares;
Settings light and pure prepare.

People gathered round in peace,
Waiting for Truth's deep release;
Spoken Word, not often heard,
Though inner, outer life is stirred.

Action stirred by Christ within;
Faith that moves people to care,
Causing them to help and share
Loads far heavier than theirs.

Hymns that rise from deep inside,
Fly like feathers to the sky,
To a God who hears them all,
Listens, bends to those who call.

Blessed be the God of peace
Who receives our hymns with grace,
Hymns that come from any place,
God wants so to share our lives!

2008

GOD, SAVE US FROM OUR GRIEVING

God, save us from our grieving, isolation;
Relieve us from our anger, desperation;
Help us emerge restored from deep depression;
Lord, help us subdue our dark obsessions.

Enter in, Spirit Divine, with loving grace;
Lift sadness from our burdened hearts and face,
Shine in darkened corners of our clouded minds;
Breathe life into our sickened souls, there find

Your true purpose for each precious, unique life;
Faith, hope, love to end our inner pain and strife;
Move us from self-absorption to new passion,
Aid those whose lives need more our deep compassion.

We thank You, God, for treasures You have stored,
Despite that we act rude and spoiled, bored;
Help us see, appreciate, with courage bear
Those whom You have brought to us for loving care.

2008

AT THE HELM AND EVER NEAR

Lord, subdue this roaring wind,
Raging wild and deep within;
Tossing the sick soul about,
Torment causing us to shout.

Shout to You, who at the helm
Can steer us to a better realm;
One that we feel so far from,
While we wait Your kingdom come.

It's the waiting we abhor!
But what are we waiting for?
Heaven on Earth, end of strife,
Evil chased, our soon rebirth?

We await the Prince of Peace,
End of war and crime to cease;
End of poverty, disease,
Hunger, chopping down of trees.

Wind, be still in the sick soul!
Help us, Lord, to become whole;
Become active for Your sake,
Help a sleeping world awake.

Awake to news that You *are* here,
At the helm and ever near;
We need be only still to see,
Your Light within us hastens Thee.

2008

THE CRISP, GREEN CALL

The crisp, green call of morning,
Drenched in sunlight after rain,
Lifts a damp dark night of ailing
From despair and body pain.

How clear dear Holy Spirit
Makes what troubled night before,
Disappear like clouds so near it;
Sun of God my life restores!

Lord, thank you for your mercy,
All your kindness, willingness,
To help, restore, rebirth us;
Life in You is blessedness.

2008

WHEN WE THINK
THAT WE MIGHT DIE

When we think that we might die,
Because some pain so frightens;
Look up to a bright blue sky
Your scared, dole face will brighten!

Eternal life starts here on Earth,
When Christ lives in your heart;
Life starts here with your rebirth,
So that when from Earth we part

We live life resurrected,
By the One who made it so;
In God's life, perfected.
Spirit helps us to let go,

Let go body made of clay,
Earth's home for soul and spirit;
God's embracing love and way,
Eternal life, why fear it!

2008

FAR WORSE THAN
DEVASTATING STORMS

Far worse than devastating storms,
Cruelty, taking many forms:
Mean words that shake our fragile worlds,
Make our crystal houses shatter.

Everybody needs to matter!
Hear gracious words that help, restore;
Restore the body, spirit, mind,
Why do we fear to just be kind?

Did not our loving Lord show grace;
Teach that love builds up, builds faith?
That when we tear down self-esteem;
We, too, tear down the Christ within?

The Christ within will bear the pain,
Caused by those minds whose petty pride,
Makes them afraid and turn aside
From those who reach in faith to them.

Lord Jesus Christ in us abides;
With love stands always by our side;
Bears words that shatter, actions cruel;
Reminds us of Love's Golden Rule.

2008

EVER WONDER HOW, WHERE, WHY?

Ever wonder how things grow,
Ask about where from creeks flow?
Why white petal blossoms blow
Pass us by like silent snow?

Nature's beauty brings such awe
Out in those who stop and pause;
Yet, we do not understand
Why her wrath takes life and land.

If God commands land, sky, sea,
Why such chaos, piled debris?
What purpose served, communities
Laid waste, destroyed, left to bleed?

We wonder at life's mysteries!
Puzzled by anxieties;
Pray day-night our fright will cease;
Ask God's help with daily needs.

Underneath our fear hope lies!
God sent His Son, heard our cries;
Brings us Home through second birth,
Life restored, Heaven on Earth!

2008

KEEP US EVER MAKING ART

Thank You, Lord, for paintings of
Images reflecting love;
Art that soars our spirits high,
Above heavy, longing sighs.

Thank You, Lord, for graceful dance
Miming out our long romance.
Thank You, too, for poems bright,
Words so sacred in your sight.

Thank You, Lord, for skits and plays,
Making music, hymns of praise,
Leading us into Your grace,
Up to You our art we raise.

Thank You, Lord, for all You bring
Out in us to make us sing;
Every soul shall have their part;
Keep us ever making art.

2008

GRACE IS TENDER, FULL OF COMPASSION

Ev'ry glint of sunlight in the creek,
Ev'ry flick'ring shadow on the grass,
Ev'ry tear of light in eye, on cheek,
Is Grace now with us, as she passes
Through worlds of pain, so torn by grief.

Grace is tender, full of compassion;
Sweeps through places, bereft by storms;
Restores our hope and selfless passion
To build anew now what was before.
Lord, forgive us, for Your love doubting!

Without God's love, life would be horror;
Without Christ Jesus, our hearts would break;
Without His grace, whom would we mirror
To dispel despair from which we ache?
God, we thank You for Life, our breathing!

Hallelujah, for the true Spirit,
Who binds, in grief, all humans living;
Binds together, all diff'ring faithful;
And fills our hearts with joyful giving.

2008

WHEN GRACE STEPS IN, SWEEPS PAIN ASIDE

When Grace steps in, sweeps pain aside,
Takes pain we suffer from our pride;
Takes away held grief from losses,
Anger, fear, all woe life tosses;

I know our Lord is present here,
Renewing what we hold so dear;
Fixing things without our doing,
Righting wrongs within us brewing.

Grace heals wrongs to make them right.
May we hold fast to Christ's pure Light;
Make peace with neighbor, self, and foe;
Hate, jealousy, pride, fear, let go.

Hold on to hope for better times,
Renewed relationships more kind.
Grace can renew what hurt has wrought;
Grace will renew the mind's ill thought.

God's grace is love, abundant, wide;
God's grace frees us, makes peace inside;
Helps us forgive, more joy to give;
Thanks be to God in whom we live!

2008

EVERYBODY HAS THEIR DAY

Sweet red flower opens up
To receive God's streaming sun;
Basks in brilliant, steaming rays
Until brightest day is done.

Dark green plant from which she comes
Will many more red flow'rs display;
I am one! You, too, are one!
Everybody has their day.

Sun and rain,
Wind and storm;
Joy and pain,
Life evermore!

2008

THE COMFORTER WHO

If I should die before you do,
I would be spared deep grieving;
What would it take to get me through,
Were you the one first leaving?

How do loved ones get through grieving
Loss of those held dear to them?
What holds them fast, keeps them breathing;
Comforts them without, within?

The Comforter who comes to heal,
Comes through the warmth of others;
Spirit of Love who makes us know
Our grief is shared by sisters, brothers.

Dear God, whose love binds sorrowed hearts,
Wrenched and torn by grief they share;
Come now, before our loved ones part,
Bring comfort, peace, help us to bear.

2008

ARE WE READY TO RECEIVE?

When we ask the Lord for mercy,
That our broken bodies heal;
When we plead to God, relieve us;
When we're hungry for a meal;

Are we ready to receive it,
That true Life for which we seek?
Do we really want Love's healing
When our lives are dark and bleak?

Would we rather live in darkness,
Deep in sorrow, dread, and pain?
Far easier to waste away,
Than to rise and walk again?

Jesus asks the simple question,
As He did the broken man:
Do you want to become whole now?
Then, in faith, just take my hand!

I will heal you, said Christ Jesus,
And provide for all your needs:
You will not again go hungry,
On the bread with which I feed.

Abundance lies before us all,
A Life of Love, Joy, Plenty;
We receive it when we're ready
To believe, forgive times seventy.

2008

HOW CAN ONE SING?

How can one fly
When there is no sky;
How can one sing
With a broken wing?
When lights grow dim,
We can rest in Him.

Have mercy, Lord
On our fearful days;
May we come to You
For peace always;
Bring concerns to You
And heart-felt praise.

2008

MY LAST BREATH WILL BE
MY SONG

You can sing when you're dancing,
You can sing when romancing;
You can sing when you're grieving,
Even sing when you're seething.

You can sing when you're crying,
You can sing when you're dying;
As long as I am breathing,
My last breath will be my song!

My last breath will be my song,
If it takes a whole day long;
Lord, I come to You with singing,
That's all I will be bringing,
Just my song.

2008

MY FAVORITE PLACE TO BE

My favorite place to be
Is in stillness, hearing Thee;
By water as it falls.
In grasses blowing tall,
In waves that splash my feet.
Inside, just where we meet.
There I hear Thee best,
Inside, when I'm at rest,
Early morn and eventide.

2008

OUR RESCUE IS GOD'S SPIRIT

When we get left behind,
Because we cannot climb
Down deep valleys, up high slopes;
What saves, renews our hopes?

Rescue by God's Spirit!
Go within, get near it,
To soar vast highs and lows;
There's no place we can't go!

Spirit life, unending!
Bodies need no mending,
Are left behind in sod,
As our spirits soar in God's.

2008

WHY HAVE US KNOW
AND FEEL GREAT PAIN?

Why have us know and feel great pain,
To teach us what it means to human be?
That we would know compassion and kind words,
Direct Your grace to folks in agony?

I have been wond'ring why must we suffer
When to be fit could serve You best?
Is it Your plan now to make us tougher,
Or more humble for rough roads ahead?

2008

TO BE ALL HUMAN IS TO SUFFER

When pain becomes far worse than we can bear,
Far worse than all we thought we could endure;
Does living then become a hell, unfair?
Are we, then, being burned to become pure?

Made pure for Heaven's God-fulfilling Light;
Leave broken bodies racked in tortuous pain?
When do our spirit bodies take their lofty flight;
Released to fly, in peace, back home again?

When might our suffering and agony
Become a blessing to our life on Earth?
When we share the plight of all humanity,
Like He who suffered, scorned, for our rebirth?

To be all human is to suffer pain!
He, who will wipe each tear from every eye,
Knows deep despair and hope for greater gain;
Promises true joy in Him who never dies.

2008

HOLY CITY, CLEAR AS CRYSTAL

Holy city, clear as crystal
Radiant jewel, transparent glass;
No more mourning, pain or crying,
Only Light through which we pass.

No more sickness, fear of dying,
No more threat of law by pistol,
No more hate or love defying,
No more hunger, thirst or past.

Only joy, behold God's glory!
Lamb of God, Son resurrected;
Earth, Heaven new: God's true story;
In Jesus Christ, we are perfected.

River of Life, bright as crystal,
Flowing downward to my soul;
Take me to God's Holy city
Where all beings become whole.

2008

SWEET SHALOM WITHIN AT LAST

Are we at peace with our condition
Or at war with self and Lord?
Have we made room for our Savior,
Trusted in His saving Word?

In Him may we live forever,
No thing can us separate,
From His love that binds and heals us,
Curing bitterness, self-hate.

Praise good God for our condition,
Sweet shalom within at last!
We will trust the Light of Jesus
To shine through the pain of past.

2008

DROP DOWN, DROP IN FROM HECTIC LIFE

Drop down, drop in from hectic life;
Steep in my healing waters deep;
Leave far above all that brings strife;
Drop down, drop in, my wisdom seek.

Drop down, drop in, come for relief;
Come find me deep within your soul;
I will comfort you with peace,
Help ease your pain, my Grace consoles.

Drop down, drop in, be still and know,
That healing comes when you come near;
My well-spring, Love's unending flow,
Will wash away shame, rage, and fear.

2008

MY HEART LEAPS UP
IN GLADNESS

When branches turn to diamonds
Sun-filled and sparkling bright;
When pine trees bend their lowest
Into snow so shining white;

My heart leaps up in gladness
Begins swelling with delight;
Feels the passing of all sadness,
Blest indwelling of Christ's Light.

2008

WAITING FOR THE CHRIST

Waiting here and staying nigh,
Watching stars, dark clouds go by;
Waiting for the Christ to come
From within or from on high.

When will raw cold nights be done;
When will we see brighter Sun?
When will streets be paved with gold;
When will hearts receive Love's flow?

Ancient star, behold the sky!
Bleating sheep out in the cold,
Waiting here and staying nigh,
To hear a blessed baby cry.

2008

PARADISE IS HERE AGAIN

Through chartreuse leaves, sunlight passes:
Golden patches, greener grasses;
Bark-brown rocks, cool wet branches;
Paradise is here again!

Through golden lashes, eyelids thin,
God's warming sunlight enters in;
Meets Christ's golden Light within.
Paradise is here again!

2008

EASTER BLOSSOMS IN MY SOUL

Easter blossoms in my soul,
Bright day of resurrection;
Life in Christ shall make us whole
In Him is full perfection.

Crutches, wheelchairs gone are they
In Heav'n where I'll be living;
Oh, that happy, happy day,
His love receiving, giving!

Into light of boundless joy
From out death's tomb I'm rising;
Round me God's green pastures lie,
New Earth, not so surprising!

2010

PURE BEAUTY

Pure beauty of the blossom
Burst in branches overhead;
This spring, new life most awesome,
Our Christ rising from the dead.

Sun rising on town houses
Warms cold hearts and rosy cheeks;
Cool shadows, hearts emblazoned,
Water dancing in bright creeks.

Outside is on my inside,
Brightest sky cerulean blue;
Wish now could last forever
Like the blushing of new bride.

2010

WHEN I HEAR BIRDS AGAIN

When I again hear birds sound spring,
And from their sweet throats sing
Of days most green and full of hope,
That round me their songs bring;

I let go deep gloom of dark,
Of winter days severely stark;
And hope for better days ahead
On roads I would embark.

Lord, for love I will then choose
Your path of Light, unused;
And listen to Your hopeful word,
And bid my sloth adieu.

Indiff'rent ways, forgive the rest,
Most lazy, I transgress;
Your way of grasping, caring love,
Bright days ahead be blest.

2010

HELP US SING SWEET HYMNS

Tears from our eyes no longer pour,
Ache in heavy heart won't heal;
Pent-up grief seeks open door,
No one knows just how we feel.

We once had light, now life is dark,
We once had joy, now joy is gone;
Gone bright flame that gave life spark,
In despair, gone heaven's song.

Hear our human cry, Christ Jesus!
Let us hear Your melody;
In this place so far from grace,
Help us sing sweet hymns again.

Your faithfulness to us in past,
Your love proves a steadfast bond;
Trust in You softens grief's blast,
Holding hope, we shall respond.

2010

GOD'S GRACE RESTORES

So silently fall flakes of snow,
To gently cover frozen ground;
Like Grace that falls on grieving hearts,
To heal pain's bruise without a sound.

Like manna falling from bleak sky,
Like water pouring from rough rock;
God's Grace restores, helps us get by,
Would that this Grace be in our walk.

Would that this Grace become our way,
Fall on all neighbors when we talk,
Cover both those we love and hate,
Make peace where e'er we go or stay.

2010

WHEN YOU GO OFF TO WAR

When you go off to war, remember me;
Keep memories of me closest to your breast;
I will pray that you more mindful be,
And be at peace should God call you to rest.

I pray that you stay safe within God's Love;
That you will feel around you my soft arms;
That horror, should it touch you, touch the Dove,
So mercy swoops to save you from all harm.

I pray to God for strength to wait and bear;
That we may have Christ's courage to endure;
[That] Community support for us be there;
God bind our love, reach over distant shores.

When you come home from war, remember me;
Those memories of me closest to your breast
May fade as we will in the present see
Ourselves anew, new memories, love's test.

Now peace and love be with you as you go;
Fear not, for God is with you in life, death.
Your sacrifice for freedom, how we owe!
May God protect your every move, thought, breath.

2010

WHEN THOSE WE LOVE

When those we love are failing
Lord, what help can we provide
To keep their lives from paling
From despair, hurt, pain inside?

As they struggle, strain to bear
Bright faces midst their ailings,
We best be Your presence there,
Compassion through sweet mailings!

Letters, phone calls, visits make,
Help to end their isolation,
Bring Your light to those in darkness,
Hope through communication.

2010

DOVE, COME DANCE WITH ME

Tree, tree, come dance with me,
Dance until the moon shakes free;
Drop soft pine leaves down on me,
In Paradise, be ever green.

Fawn, fawn, come dance with me,
Dance until all fright is gone;
Leap with courage into dawn,
In Paradise, we shall be free.

Snow, snow, come dance with me,
Dance until my world is white;
Drop soft flakes upon my face,
Paradise is Peace, Grace, Light.

Dove, Dove, come dance with me,
Dance until realm from above
Becomes a pure religion here,
One of love, compassion, cheer.

2010

MAY YOUR LOVE

My weary soul seeks greater cause,
Longs for a Life of passion,
Connection to a world so flawed,
That I could find new mission.

Spirit, move me into action,
So that I may sense God's call;
May Your love be my distraction
Keep me safe from evil's fall.

Where You lead me, I will follow,
Even "Bloom where planted," bear;
Keep me from a life that's hollow,
Ope my heart, there's music there.

2010

EMANUEL, OUR LIGHT

Silently soft snow is falling,
Children, hear your mothers calling
Go to bed, to prayers, to sleeping.
This is Christmas Eve, no peeping.

Christ is come; He hears your weeping,
Knows your pain, your secrets keeping;
Stands beside, above, below you,
Stands behind and walks before you.

Emanuel, our Light from heaven;
Protector, guide whom God has given
To lead us out of death's darkness
Into bright Life of blessedness.

2009

WHEN HOLIDAYS SEEM

When holidays to us seem bittersweet
Because loved ones are sick or slowly dying,
Distant, or lost or living in dark streets,
And we can't keep our best selves from crying,

Thank Grace for being present with sad feelings,
Our numbness, disbelief, god-rage, fear, pain;
This downward spin from which we are now reeling
Will subside in time, yet may occur again.

Who will help us heal in times of grieving?
Christ, who bears our trials and deep sorrows;
Christ, who's always with us, never leaving;
Christ, here today, yesterday, tomorrow.

2009

OF FLAPPING WINGS AND WATERFALLS

Awake, my heart, to morning call
Of flapping wings and waterfalls;
Here in this wild where life is raw,
I stand before You, still, in awe
Of natural things, both large and small,
All bright and dull, cherish them all:

Breathe in the scent of evergreens,
Crunch down dry leaves, earth damp and clean,
Sing with delight as turkeys preen;
Take in wild pumpkins, corn, and beans,
To know God's holiness in these,
Is Heaven here, in beauty seen!

2009

THE DAY IS COMING

Come Holy Light, my conscious soul
Awakens on this golden morn;
Moments of Grace, joyful and whole,
Despite days dark, lost, and forlorn.

Advent approaches in the cells
Of body bent and woeful torn;
Bring in the branch of pine-green smells,
The day is coming of the Lord.

Go light the fires, prepare the feasts,
Go bring in neighbors far and near;
Haul in the hay for hairy beasts,
Christ's birthing day is almost here!

2010

SHALOM NOW BIND US

Before You we are kneeling,
Shalom, Lord, bring Your healing
To where harsh violence is
Killing children's innocence.

Together we are praying,
Let children keep on playing,
Among a new creation
Safe, sound in every nation.

Let Your Shalom now bind us,
Put killing far behind us,
We beg for Your forgiveness,
May Your grace renew, transform us.

2009

HEART SOARING

Line my pine box with nettles soft,
Then lay me in the ground,
Where I may ease and merge with earth,
My spirit free, unbound;

To rise and fly through Heaven's door
To be embraced by Thee;
To leave behind a body worn,
Behind, among wet leaves.

But, oh that door bids me while here!
Your Life gives me wide wings;
For You, dear Christ, are ever near,
Heart soaring, Your grace brings.

2009

RADIANT PETALS

Yellow flower bright as Sun,
Radiant petals touching me;
In me has new life begun,
As I cast all thought to Christ.

Dark green leaves, sharp-edged and rough,
Not soft petals blessing me,
More like sandy crust to touch,
Like the shell encasing me.

Lord,
Crack this crust so I may be,
Right to those who reach to me.

2009

COOL GREEN GLADE

Cool green glade, refresh my soul,
Crystal creek flow, make me whole,
Wash away sludge of my sin,
Cool green glade, my shade within.

Cool soft wind, refresh my mind,
Holy Spirit, I am Thine,
Blow away all selfish thought,
Let my life be Spirit taught (bought).

2009

MERCY ON YOUR CREATURES

Harbinger of morning Light,
Dipping, soaring gold-tipped wings;
How I envy joyous flight!
I wake broken from dark night,
Worried with so many things
Gone awry, out of control;
Tortured body, tortured soul.

Yet, I know you suffer too.
Brave harsh elements, harsh wild.
We are both beloved, God's child,
Made for heaven when we die.
Yet what differs me from you
In harsh times, you still can sing;
I still worry, stuck, can't fly.

Mercy on your creatures, Lord!
Grace to those on leg or wing;
Grace to those of scale and fin;
Peace on Earth, end pain, grief, sin;
Your world, help us enter in.
We praise You for giving life,
Being near through ease and strife.

2010

NEW EARTH

Dandelions dot green grass,
Glitter sparkles in far creek;
Narrow gate through which I pass,
Leads me to blest land I seek.

Season of delights foretold,
Wine and bread, fine table spread;
All are welcome, young and old,
Rich and poor to host be led.

Hallelu, baptismal font,
Sweetest creek that I dip in;
Ne'er again shall any want,
Cry, feel pain, or hurt from sin.

2010

CHRIST-LIGHT BREAKING

Birds are waking, sudden breeze;
Storm in making, on this morn.
Leaves are shaking down from trees;
Earth is quaking, veil is torn!

Christ-light breaking, fall on knees;
Old Earth dimming, bright Earth born.
None are sinning, all at ease;
Playing, singing, none forlorn.

2010

WE ARE ONE

Church bells ringing,
Songbirds singing,
Calling us to worship God.

Prophets naming
Game we're playing,
Bringing fire, flood, disease.

Our salvation?
Be God's people,
Turn to justice, love, and peace.

Flee to temple,
House with steeple,
Flock to synagogue or mosque.

Breathe God's Spirit,
That unites us:
We are one, yes, we are one.

2010

WHILE DOLPHINS DIE

Red birds feast in berry tree,
While dolphins die in oily sea;
God, forgive us for our greed,
Selfish ways and gross misdeeds.

When will we awake from sleep,
Honor Earth, Commandments keep?
When we suffer, bleed, and grieve,
Turn to You, repent, believe?

How much grieving must we bear
For Your trust that we still care?
Will we ever get it right,
Shine Your image, be Your Light?

Care for Brothers, Sisters, Earth?
Walk Your way where crossroads merge?
Evil from our sins, Lord, purge;
Peace, love, joy, sweet song rebirth!

2010

MORNING LIGHT

Cut crystal glass, facets of Light,
Sun sparks through ice on frozen boughs;
Seen dancing on a bright blue sea,
Seen dancing on a gladed stream;

Seen caught through leaves wet, dark, and green;
My Morning Light, without, within,
Your sparkle changes me again,
Your sparkle lights a spark in me.

2010

MY CHILDREN ARE IN HEAVEN

My children are in Heaven;
They never entered here;
They were already perfect,
Bright, healthy, happy, whole.

They wait for me to find them;
They stand by heaven's gate,
With my old dogs and kittens,
Who met their earth-bound fate;

With those who went before me,
Those whom I loved so dear;
The party is in Heaven,
So what have I to fear?

I have come to be at peace
In body, mind, and soul;
My heart already with them,
As my end years draw near.

2010

GRIEF HELD DEEP

Grief held deep within the soul,
Held hard, often for many years,
Surprises us when up it swells,
Bursts out in sobs or gentle tears.

Grief swells up when memory
Reminds the heart of what is lost;
Or when we taste some of what was,
Remember, sadly, bitter cost.

Yet from ashes phoenix rises,
From cross and grave our Lord appears;
God making new of all that died,
Love bringing joy to painful years.

2010

YOU STILL ARE THERE

When our hearts break,
You still are there;
When we cry out
In deep despair,
Still You are there,
Still You are there.

When we feel left,
Bereft, alone;
When far from Home,
Still You are there,
Still You are there.

You still are there
To comfort, care,
Hold us in prayer,
When hope is dim,
You still are there.

When You seem gone,
Our souls are bared,
You still are there
Still holding on;
You are still there.

2010

AS I NOW LIE UPON MY BED

As I now lie upon my bed,
Outside my windows see
Large stalwart oaks, their limbs low bent
Swaying with faded leaves.

Evergreens, tall grass, fall weeds
Praise dancing in morn's light;
And those who pray for me to heal
Are angels of my night;

Restoring my insight into
This dreadful malady
That makes my own small world surreal,
From one I would take flight.

How do I feel, friends ask me now;
I say, God's left my side.
They say, God comes through those who care,
That patient I must be.

I had forgotten God indwells;
In us, God's pow'r resides.
Our strength comes from who loves us most,
Faithful, our God will be.

'Til we come home to Heaven's door,
Are lovingly received;
Freed from fear, death, harsh disease,
Tears wiped dry, pain no more.

2010

GOD'S LOVE CHASTENING

Still, sitting here in silent peace,
Snowed in, wrapped warm, pain free;
I thank God's love for healing me
However slow Love's course may be.

So patiently, I wait to know
Right reason for this chastening;
To strip me clean of habits low?
To speed God's plan for hastening

My turn from satiating self
To selfless path of greater wealth?
Servant to those suffering,
So helpless in recovering?

If I may offer hope to them,
As one who walks their road of pain,
I would do it all again,
Succumb to God's love chastening!

2011

BURY ME NOW

Let me lie angelic in this snow
That has buried all I know;
Bury me now, freeze my bliss,
Let each flake become a kiss
That smothers breath,
Brings painless death,
Takes me to a frozen sleep,
And wakes me up in Paradise
In the Heart of Love, Joy, Peace.

2011

CRYSTAL LIFE

Crystal Life is calling me;
Beauty in deformity;
Love around us falling free,
Like ice melting on far tree.

Hearts will melt more easily
When God's grace evokes mercy
For those suff'ring endlessly;
Crystal Life is calling me.

Crystal Life is calling me,
Calling me to look to see
Deep into humanity
For near Christ, Divinity.

2011

CRYSTAL CROSS

Crystal cross melt into water,
Draught of Life down from the Sun;
Flowing under snow He caught her,
Where her dying had begun.

Up she comes into bright Sunlight,
Gasping air (she had succumbed);
Oh, deep draught of Life will bear her,
On beyond when earth days done.

Refrain:
Sing new life from old life rising,
Praise pure Presence of our Lord.

2011

SOMEBODY'S PRAYING

Somebody's prayin' hard for me,
For in the dark God's angels came;
Now I've got trust, faith, hope again,
My life will never be the same.

For in the dark white butterflies
Appeared and circled round my head,
Shaped like dear angels in disguise,
I lay half dead upon my bed.

Their mini, bright angelic wings,
Fluttered around my opened eyes;
Such silent grace their hoverings,
Deep peace came to me by surprise.

Such Love bestowed flowed through my corpse,
Assuring health, my wellbeing;
I let go guilt, fear, tears, remorse,
That hindered my recovering.

Somebody's prayin' hard for me,
For in the dark God's angels came;
Now I've got trust, faith, hope again,
My life will never be the same.

2011

JUST BE

Let the inner battle die,
Mute the ego's battle cry,
Rest the question who am I,
Keep God's healing peace inside,
Just be.

Just be who you're meant to be,
Child of God, forever free,
In the Life given for thee,
By the One nailed to a tree,
Just be.

When your fever to be best,
Separates you from the rest,
God will then provide the test,
Bring you back into her nest,
Just be,
Just be,
Just be!

2011

FLOWER SO BLUE

Flower so blue that through her I saw Heaven;
Creatures, human and non, glimpses of Holy,
Some more pure like Jesus bring us vision
Of what ought to be our mission here. Like:

Kindness out of love and not of duty;
Like caring out of sharing, not of guilt.
Heart to heart remove deep pain of feelings
That have clouded, veiled our purer sight.

"Heaven is within," said our Lord Jesus;
Follow Him and you will see God's Light.
Joy will spring from Conscious evolution,
New Earth will then appear within, without.

Flower so blue that through her I see Heaven.
Grass so green from rain I, too, wash clean.
Birds whose simple songs pierce even deeper
Than wisest words of high and holy priests!

2011

EMERALD LEAF, INVITE ME IN

Emerald leaf, invite me in
To your world of chartreuse light;
Ocean wide, invite me in
To your world of layered blue.

Frightened child, invite me in
To your world of dismal night;
Christ in me is reaching out,
Wanting to invest in you:

Wanting me to be His eyes,
Wanting me to be His hands,
Wanting me to hear your cries,
Wanting me to take a stand,

Wanting me to make the choice
To be silent or His voice.
Christ in me is reaching out,
Wanting to invest in you.

2011

NEW WORLD'S COMIN'

New world's comin', I see glory!
Someone's list'nin' to our story.
Change is comin', Earth is turnin',
Fields are floodin', hills are burnin'.

Listen to the sound of Heaven
Make her way through nature singin',
Make her way through people carin',
Make her way through people sharin'.

New world's comin', I see glory!
Someone's list'nin' to our story.

2011

SAVIOR, HOLY SPIRIT

I cannot save my sister,
I cannot save my brother,
I cannot save my father,
I cannot save my mother.

I cannot save my nieces,
Uncles, aunts, or friends,
My spouse or any other,
So I look to Him who can.

Can, because He hears me,
Harkens to my pleading,
Wonders why I worry,
Knows my heart is bleeding.

Savior, Holy Spirit,
Who saves through love and grace,
May we know Your leading
Help us to be Your face.

Your face to each encounter,
Each person brought our way,
Your voice to those in places
Where silence screams today.

2011

ADVENT IS HERE

When pine trees blow,
When scent of snow,
When God I know
From center flows;
Advent is here,
His birth is near.

When joy springs forth
From place of pain,
I know that I
Am whole again;
Advent is here,
My sight is clear.

My Savior dear
Has wiped my tears,
Has come into
My heart again.
Advent is here,
New life, New Year.

2011

FROM GOD'S HEART THERE FLOWS A RIVER (Ezekiel 47:1, 3–12)

From God's heart there flows a river,
Flows a river ankle deep;
On dry banks roots that had withered,
Wake to nourish trees asleep.

From God's heart a river's flowing,
Flowing higher to my knees;
On moist banks flowers are growing,
Shooting out their new green leaves.

From God's heart a river's rising,
Over waist above my head;
What I find ev'n more surprising,
Fruit from trees that once were dead.

I cannot now cross this river,
Will swim in her flow instead;
When she reaches stagnant ocean,
She will make stale ocean fresh.

Fish of diff'rent kinds will be there,
Fish for filling spreading nets;
Creatures weak will soon revive there,
Stagnant swamps for salt be left.

From God's heart a healing river,
Love and Justice is her name;
Joy is swimming where she's going,
Bright new Earth, Heaven's domain.

2010

My Emerald Leaf, Paradise Within

From God's Heart There Flows a River

1. From God's heart there flows a river, flows a river an'-kle deep,
2. From God's heart a ri-ver's flow-ing, flowing high-er to my knees,
3. From God's heart a ri-ver's ri-sing, ov-er waist, a-bove my head,
4. I can not now cross this ri-ver, will swim in her flow in-stead,
5. Fish of diff-rent kinds will be there, fish for fill-ing spread-ing nets,

1. On dry banks roots that had with-erd, wake to nou-rish trees a-sleep,
2. On moist banks flow-ers grow-ing, shoo-ting out their new green leaves,
3. What I find ev'n more sur-pri-sing, fruit from trees that once were dead,
4. When she rea-ches stag-nant o-cean, she will make stale o-cean fresh,
5. Crea-tures weak will soon re-vive there, stag-nant swamps for salt be left,

6. From God's heart a healing river
Love and justice is her name.
Joy is swimming where she's going
Bright new Earth, Heaven's domain.

"Omni dei"
8.7.8.7

Words: Sandy Smyth, © 2010.
Based on Ezekiel 47:1,3-12.
Music: Gross Catolisch Gesangbuch,
Nurnberg, 1631; arr. William Smith Rockstro, 1823-1895.

230

PART V.

MORE FRIENDS' PRAYER STORIES

Words Will Be Given

In 1988 I was asked to go to Ecuador to attend the dedication of a new church that had been funded by our parish. I jumped at the chance for this wonderful, new experience. There were five other people on the trip. Four of them were from the diocese and had different functions representing the bishop. In the group we had only one person who spoke Spanish. He, Andy, was also our only priest.

We had been told the Spirit of God was vibrantly alive in Ecuador, and we saw it first hand. We spent most of the week in small towns and jungle villages visiting Episcopal churches and meeting local priests, families, and many barefooted children. During our nightly prayer meeting in a room with open windows, a monkey climbed through the window to join us.

The night before the dedication, we were invited to dine at the bishop's house. The evening turned out to be very festive, and the bishop was in fine fettle. As we left, he was explaining the directions to us regarding the next day's service. At one point he said, "And Patty will give the sermon." We all had a good chuckle over that, knowing that Andy was on the docket for the sermon, since he was the only Spanish-speaking member of the group.

The appointed time for the dedication arrived and, of course, the temperature hovered around 100 degrees in the city with no AC. Our group was led to the front of the church and given seats behind the altar, facing the congregation. The service started all in Spanish with the bishop presiding. Someone handed us programs printed in English. Andy nudged me and pointed to something on the paper. It read: "Sermon – Patty." I froze, unable to function. No way could I do that!! My few Spanish words would hardly make a sentence, let alone a sermon. At that time the Gospel was being read. Andy told me that the reading was about the sower and the seeds falling on different types of ground (Mark 13:3–9).

I said a brief prayer, something like, "OK, God. You put me here. DO SOMETHING!" I grabbed Andy, and together we walked to the microphone. I spoke, and he translated into Spanish. Only because I have a tape of the sermon do I remember what I said. I have listened to the tape and recognize my own voice. However, the words were God's—NOT MINE.

"Do not worry about how you are to speak or what you are to say; for what you are to say will be given to you at that time; for it is not you who speak, but the Spirit of your Father speaking through you (Matthew 10:19–20).

A Wife's Story

No matter how old we are, we are never ready to lose our mothers. As hard as it is, there are always rays of sunbeams at times like that. When my father-in-law passed away, we went back to his home, and there was a baby buck staring right at me. (I called my father-in-law "Buck.") To me, he was telling me that it was all right. I had never seen a buck there before, and never have since then. There was also the most beautiful sunrise when we came out of the nursing home. All were messages from God.

But the story I want to relate, which illustrates how God works in our lives when we live in a responsive, prayerful relationship with Him, is when my husband was in the Air

Force and was trying to get hired by the airlines. In 1972, Steve enlisted in the Air Force. We had been teaching a fifth-grade Sunday school class in Columbus, Ohio, and the lesson called for cutting articles from a newspaper. That Sunday morning, there was a full-page ad to join the Air Force Reserves. When I saw it, I showed it to my husband, who had his private pilot's license and loved flying. We were at a crossroads in our careers. He decided to enlist, but our mothers were not happy.

They jumped into their car and drove the 90 miles from Lima, Ohio, to Columbus to try to talk him out of enlisting. The Vietnam War was in full swing at the time. But, Steve was adamant—he had friends who were drafted because their families could not afford to send them to college, and he felt that was wrong. Steve enlisted for the Air Force RESERVES, but somehow, his paperwork was sent to the REGULAR Air Force, so we were committed for 6½ years. But that was OK with us. We decided to start our family then since the Air Force would pay all medical expenses, and his salary was more than double what we had been making.

When he was in pilot training, he was told that he could choose his assignment (plane) according to his class rank. Then two weeks before graduation, they announced that the top ten percent would be made instructor pilots. Steve's choice assignment, an RF4 to Germany, went to the last guy in the class. That was the beginning of the end of his Air Force career. There were many other "changes" that disillusioned him, so Steve decided NOT to train in another aircraft and add additional years to his commitment.

In 1976 we were in San Antonio, where Steve trained instructor pilots at Randolph AFB. The Air Force came out with a new policy so that a pilot could resign his commission, but he would be in the reserves for the additional time if they needed him. After the Vietnam War, there were too many pilots, and it was too costly for the government. So

Steve applied to Braniff Airlines, and he was hired. We were thrilled. We could stay in San Antonio where we were active in our church and had many friends.

But, suddenly, the Air Force realized that they had let too many pilots go, and they discontinued Palace Chase and Palace Furlough (the two programs to release AF pilots for their commission). We were so disappointed. We sat by and watched hundreds of pilots being hired every month by Braniff. But, we were stuck in the Air Force for two more years, an eternity to us!

I was in Bible Study Fellowship at the time, and we kept reading Psalm 27:14: "Wait thou, and be patient in the Lord." We were waiting, and we were being patient, but this was NOT working out! Then, the Air Force adopted a policy that if a pilot refused his assignment, he would be automatically discharged. We lived across the street from a general in the Military Personnel Center, and he told Steve that he would get him any plane that he wanted to fly. Steve was assigned an RF4 to Shaw AFB in South Carolina, which he refused (his Dream Airplane), but the Air Force had once again changed their policy, and we couldn't get out of his commitment. We were so frustrated. We were being patient, but this was NOT working out!

Finally, in March 1979, Steve was eligible to be released from the Air Force. In January Braniff had hired 500 pilots; in February, just a few; and in March, no one. When Steve contacted the vice president who had hired him previously at Braniff, he was gone. No one would help us at Braniff. But, every door opened at American Airlines. I had a dream that Steve would be hired by an airline based in Nashville, Tennessee. The next morning I looked at a chart of airline bases, and American Airlines was the only airline that had a base in Nashville. I took that as a sign from God. American was also the only airline that flew to Dayton, Ohio, the closest major airport to Lima, Ohio.

Steve was hired by American, and a few years later, Braniff was bankrupt and no longer flying. In July 2011, Steve retired from American after 32 years. He had a premonition that it was the right time. In July, only a handful of pilots retired, but on November 29, 2011, American Airlines declared bankruptcy also. We had a wonderful "ride" with American, protected by God.

A Daughter's Story

My mom was very religious and prayed a lot. Most days she said the rosary during the day or before she went to sleep. It took a while to sink in, but I finally realized that every morning when she opened her eyes, her first comments were, "Thank You, Lord, for another beautiful day." She had a lot of gratitude for Him and thanked Him profusely for being able to have brain cancer on the side of the brain that allowed her to speak and remember her memories. She saw others with strokes and other diseases who were not able to speak and she saw their frustration in not being able to speak or write or remember people. She was VERY grateful to be able to vocalize her thoughts and retrieve her memories without a problem.

Making a Decision

Several years ago I was faced with a major decision-making crisis. I had been doing a breast cancer "Making Strides" walk for over 13 years. It always fell on the third Sunday in October. Well, suddenly my husband received an invitation from a cousin he hadn't seen in many years whose daughter was getting married—on the third Sunday in October! Well, you can only imagine the arguments that followed as I wasn't missing my walk—and he wasn't missing the wedding, and I was going with him!

The Cancer Society would always have kick-off break-fasts, many that I didn't attend. But something made me go that day, and there I found out that they miraculously changed the date of the walk to the second Sunday in October for that year only. I left, went to my car, sat there, and just cried. God made it happen so that I could do both. I promised that I would make it up to Him by making Him a larger part of my life. I have kept my promise!

A Minister's Favorite Prayer

I believe that God answers every one of our prayers. Sometimes the answer is "yes," sometimes it's "no," and sometimes it's "maybe" or even "probably, but not yet." We often say that God doesn't answer our prayers, when what we really mean is God didn't say "yes" right away, and we hate that.

There is one prayer I use a lot, and it is answered every time. When I am confused or in trouble, not knowing what to think or do, I pray, "Help!" No fancy words, no deep insights, no instructions for God, no specific expectations. God has some room to maneuver without me directing traffic. And, without fail, God responds. Always.

My mood may change and lighten, I may suddenly see a situation clearly, or someone else or something else may shift and transform everything. But it always works. And you know what? The weirdest thing of all is that God's help seems to be at hand even when sometimes I actually forget to pray that magical and mystical prayer when I'm in trouble, despite my knowing how wonderfully it works.

Helping Hands

I hadn't grown up in a church family and had had no instruction in the Christian faith. But somehow, I had an experience of the helping hands of Jesus when I was 15 years old.

I'd been on a summer vacation in the mountains with my parents, and we had stopped in a little mountain valley for the night. It was a perfect afternoon, so after we unpacked, the three of us set off on a hike up the side of the valley to the west. After walking for 45 minutes or so, my parents turned back. I said I'd keep going for a while. I hiked a little higher, and then I turned to the south to walk back along the clear mountain stream that I could see just over the edge of the hill. I reached the stream and followed it, hopping from rock to rock as the water danced down the mountainside.

For about half an hour I made good progress back down the valley so I could join my parents for dinner. But then I came to a point where the stream plunged over a sheer precipice right in front of me. I couldn't go that way. "Uh oh," I thought, "if I have to walk all the way back upstream to where I came from, I'll be really late, and Mom and Dad will be worried." So I looked to either side to see if I could go around the waterfall. But I realized that the stream and I had gradually descended together into a small canyon with sheer walls rising up above me on both sides.

I couldn't go forward. It would take too long to go back. There was a sheer rock wall on the left that I couldn't climb. So my best bet was to go up the canyon wall on the right. This side of the canyon wasn't rocky like the other, but was a steep wall of earth with scrubby clumps of grass and bits of bushes clinging on by slender roots. I started clambering up, digging the soft toes of my sneakers into the muddy earth and grabbing on to the willow bushes and tufts of grass to pull myself up.

For about 20 feet, I did pretty well. Then I came to a place where the cliff wall became even steeper, the toe holds in the mud even slipperier, and the clumps of grass even more tenuously rooted. Suddenly, I was petrified. A vision flashed before my eyes of me having slipped and fallen down to the bottom, lying on the rocks below with a broken leg. I knew this was what was coming next.

Suddenly, from I don't know where, the words burst from my lips, "Help me, Jesus!" To this day, I don't know where in my unchurched life those words came from. But somehow, I was steadied and able to climb the rest of the way to the top of the cliff with no difficulty at all. I stood at the top, quivering with fear, looking back down at where I might I have been. "Thank you."

Within a moment, I had found a new path, and 15 minutes later, I rejoined my parents. I still wonder just what happened that day in the mountains.

A Love Story

During one of my darkest times I felt so unloved and that I was a failure at relationships, having gone through a divorce and then found a man who I felt was the one. We had a shot-gun marriage and then after three weeks he told me he had made a mistake in marrying me and was in love with another woman. So that was divorce two.

One night alone and despairing in my nearly empty house, I went on my knees and asked God to send me someone with whom I could spend the rest of my life. The next day as I left my psychologist's office, I saw a friend of mine who was there to paint her house. I invited him over to dinner (my psychologist told me to reach out to friends). We had dinner and went for a walk in the night.

Later as we sat in front of the fireplace, he told me that I was "the most beautiful woman he had ever seen." Our relationship started then, and I never forget to thank God for bringing him to me. He is my emotional rock. We had some difficult times as our relationship forced both of us to look at our shortcomings and do something about it. We have stayed together and have been supportive and happy for 26 years.

A Light Blazes in the Night

It was two o'clock in the morning at an apartment building in New York City where I was awaiting word that my youngest child had delivered her first little baby. I had heard seven hours earlier that she was in labor and that I would be hearing soon from my son-in-law. I was restless, couldn't sleep, and was convincing myself that something had happened during the delivery. Why wasn't Jim calling me?

I know — he was on his way home so that he could deliver the bad news to me personally rather than over the phone. What could I do in the meantime?

I COULD PRAY. I went to the living room window, pulled back the drapes, and looked out, from 15 stories high, at the city in darkness. The words flowed easily, as tears rolled from my eyes, praying that I would hear soon that my baby had delivered her baby and that all was OK.

With that I watched as a Roman candle was launched into the dark sky from a roof top several streets away. It was then I believed that God had heard my prayer and it was His way of telling me that the miracle of new birth had happened. Within minutes, the call came from a room at Roosevelt Hospital where my daughter was holding her baby girl and saying, "Hi, Grandma."

I couldn't get back to that picture window fast enough to offer a prayer of thanks for the wondrous event that had just taken place. That was almost 19 years ago, and I am ever mindful of that personal experience of God in my life.

My Aunt June

The most memorable and personal experience of God in my life came on the night my sister and dearest friend, June, died, on April 2, 2007. I was at my sister's bedside at a hospice home in Florida waiting for her breathing to become shallow and stop altogether. My cell phone rang, indicating it was my daughter, Kim, calling from Connecticut. She wanted news but also wanted to tell me that her son, Spencer, then age seven, was visibly upset about the pending passing of "Aunt June."

Spencer didn't know June all that well because he lived in Connecticut and she lived in Florida, but they seemed to have had a special connection through telephone calls and notes and occasional visits. I spoke to him on the phone and told him that although June couldn't speak to him, I would hold the phone up to her ear so that he could speak to her if he wanted to. His little voice quivered when he answered, "Yes." I held the earpiece away from her ear a little so that I could hear what he was saying to her with a tearful voice. His words were, "I love you, Aunt June. We all love you."

That was around 7 p.m., and June passed about an hour later. That night as Kim was putting Spencer to bed, he told her that he was seeing Aunt June up in the corner of his eye. It wasn't a dream. He was fully awake. He went on to say that she was on a football field and a white-haired man was hiking the ball to her. He described the play as she ran toward the goal line and became very excited because he watched her make a touchdown.

Every family member had a different interpretation of what Spencer's bedtime experience meant, mine being that as June was making that touchdown, she was actually being greeted at the "Pearly Gates," the name she often used when referring to Heaven. My explanation for the white-haired man was that it was her late, very white-haired husband Ken, who had predeceased her by many years.

Fast forward to many months later when I decided to present a picture to Spencer of Ken and just ask out of curiosity if the man in the picture looked familiar. It's important to know that Spencer never saw Ken because he died in 1989, nor had he ever seen a picture of him. I doubt he had ever even heard his name since he had died 17 years earlier.

Spencer studied the picture for only a few seconds and then announced that the man in the photo was the same man who had hiked the ball to Aunt June on the football field. My daughter, Kim, and I just looked at each other with bugged eyes and gasped voices, saying, "Are you sure? Are you sure?" There was no doubt in this little boy's voice. He was sure!

The sign that I had asked my sister to send me had already been sent to me through Spencer on the night she died and then again at the moment he recognized the man with the white hair. June was a wonderful, loving, devoted, pious, caring, retired nurse in her earthly days, and if any one deserved to go to Heaven and be with her benevolent God, it was she.

To emphasize Spencer's connection to June, even though he was only seven years old at the time, I should mention that one day his mother heard him talking to someone in the kitchen, and when she inquired from another room about who he was talking to, his response was, "I'm talking to Aunt June." Another time when his mom found him sitting out in the backyard looking kind of down, she asked him why he looked so blue. He said, "I'm just thinking of Aunt June and feeling sad."

There is one more "meaningful coincidence" to this story. June's funeral service was held the day before Easter Sunday. Her granddaughter-in-law, who would have been making June a great-grandmother had she lived a few weeks longer, was about five weeks short of her delivery date. She left the reception early not feeling well and promptly delivered a premature but healthy baby very early Easter morning, the day of the Resurrection, and five weeks before her scheduled due date. Was that another sign from June?

CREDITS AND REFERENCES

Introduction:

Chopra, Deepak, M.D. "Focused Intention," Deepak Chopra, keynote speaker at the 1998 Business and Consciousness Conference in Puerto Vallarta, Mexico. Compared focused intention to focused prayer when asked by this author if they were the same thing.

Jung, Carl G. (2009). *The Red Book*, edited and introduced by Sonu Shamdasani and translated by Mark Kyburz, John Peck, and Sonu Shamdasani, Philemon Series. New York, NY: WW Norton.

Tillich, Paul (1952). *The Courage to Be*. New Haven, CT: Yale University Press.

Trine, Ralph Waldo (1927). *In Tune with the Infinite*. New York, NY: Dodd, Mead and Company. In the public domain, © 1892.

Underhill, Evelyn (1926). *Concerning the Inner Life*. New York, NY: E.P. Dutton & Company, Inc.

Friends' Stories of Answered Prayer:

Alice Crowther
Alice Mindrum
Barbara Browning
Jeanne Eleck
Jolysa Sedgwick
Judy Volpe
LaWynn Murphy
Linda DePonte
Patty Moore
Shalynn Sedgwick
Stephen Blackmer

Editing:
Cathy Gilstrap

Inspiration for book:
Mae Williams
Cat Caracelo
Carla Dietz-Carroll
Stephen Blackmer

Hymn setting "Omni Dei" is from *The Hymnal 1982,* according to the use of The Episcopal Church; The Church Hymnal Corporation, New York, NY.

CPSIA information can be obtained at www.ICGtesting.com
Printed in the USA
LVOW081339130512

281478LV00003B/2/P